CLASSIFYING WITH DEWEY DECIMAL CLASSIFICATION

(Editions 19 and 20)

CLASSIFYING WITH DEWEY DECIMAL CLASSIFICATION

(Editions 19 and 20)

PUSHPA DHYANI

Ess Ess Publications

4837/24, Ansari Road, Darya Ganj,
New Delhi-110002
✆ : 3260807, 3201533
Fax : 3274173
E-mail: essess@del3.vsnl.net.in
url:http://www.essessbooks.com

First Published 2002

ISBN : 81-7000-326-1

Price : Rs. 650/-

Published by:

Ess Ess Publications

4837/24, Ansari Road, Darya Ganj,
New Delhi - 110 002
Phone : 3260807
Fax : 3274173
E-mail : essess@del3.vsnl.net.in
url: http://www.essessbooks.com

Laser Typesetting:

Mukesh Graphics

L-2/8, Mangolepuri, New Delhi
Ph.:7924405

Printed at :

Print Line

Dedicated to

MELVILL LOUIS KOSSUTH DEWEY
The Poineering Classificationist
Who Heralded A New Era
In
Library Classification

CONTENTS

PREFACE

Dewey Decimal Classification has also become by-word for library Classification. Overcoming all the hurdles of myraid canopy of subjects since 1876 to 2001, the Scheme has shined both in its compactness, world-wide popularity and usefulness. Although, it is founded on an enumerative pattern, using only ten Indo-Arabic numerals, it is trying systematically and tactically to accommodate in its number building procedure the multifacted pattern of the ever growing Universe of Subjects. However, the notation of the Scheme has remained as simple as it was in 1876 when its first edition was published. Moreover, it is also criditable that among all the existing classification schemes, it is the only Scheme which is being used in all types of libraries from small to big and general to special all over the world.

The 42 pages scheme has now grown to 4126 pages which is clear indicator that it is keeping pace with ever growing universe of subjects, in order to cope with the needs of documents *vis-a-vis* the useres. To accommodate the evergrowing complex subjects in the scheme with using just 10 numerals, the number building process has become simultaneously complex and difficult. Therefore, those who are well versed with the theory and practice of the Scheme can guide those readers who are eager to know:-

(a) the difference between the previous and the current edition to decide about the efficacy of changing from the old to the new edition;

(b) the exact specific subjects and places where the new edition departs from the old one;

(c) the new features of the new edition, together with their use and application; and

(d) *a systematic step-wise practical manual in a simple language* which may help in devising the class number using various methods provided in DDC.

In India mainly Edition 19 is being used in all types of libraries. Although, with every new edition of DDC various practical works on DDC are written by scholars of library classification, but there is not a single systematic work available which may provide guidence to those who want to change from Editions 19 to 20.

As the core content of this work is based on Editions 19 and 20, it will be equally useful to those librarians and information scientists who are involved in the difficult task of knowledge management *vis-a-vis* the library science community of academics - teachers and students whether regular or of distance education interested in the dynamics of DDC or in understanding its practical nuances.

The author acknowledges the sincere efforts of Shri Sumit Sethi of Ess Ess Publications, New Delhi in bringing out this Publication.

Nov. 2001

Dr. Pushpa Dhyani,
MA, MLibs, Ph.D.
253 Panditwari, Phase II
Dehradun - 248007.

I

THE SCHEME : GENERAL PERSPECTIVE

Melville Louis Kossuth Dewey was born on December 10, 1851 in Adams Centre, New York. In the year 1870, he joined Amherst College and graduated in 1874. He also worked as part - time assistant in the college library from 1872 and became full-time Assistant College Librarian in 1874. In 1873, he prepared the plan of Decimal Classification which was used for classifying documents of the library. The first edition of Scheme entitled. 'A Classification and Subject Index for Cataloguing and Arranging the Books and Pamphlets of a Library' was published in 1876. However, Dewey's name appeared only on the back of the title page under copyright. It was only from the second edition (1885) of DDC that Dewey's name was used as author of the Scheme. The first edition was published in the form of small book of 44 pages, which contained 1 - 10 pages preface, 11 - 22 pages Tables in which only 1000 divisions were enumerated, 23-40 pages Subject Index, 41-42 pages Explanations and 43-44 pages Subject Catalogue. However, every successive edition of DDC was so revised and modified that it increased both in content and size[1]. The edition 15 (1951) was termed as 'Standard Edition', as it was virtually an abridged edition and useful only for medium size general libraries. The Edition 16 (1958) was, therefore, published keeping in view the needs of both large and small libraries. It appeared in two volumes:-Volume 1 - Table and Volume 2 - Relative Index. To accommodate the ever growing Universe of subjects the new numbers are interpolated which has resulted in the increase of number of volumes. Editions 18 and 19 were published in three volumes and Editions 20 and 21 in four volumes.

Each new edition of DDC is being revised and modified using the latest techniques and devices developed in the field of

---

For detail *see* Library Classification; Theory and Principle by Pushpa Dhyani, Wishwa Prakashan. PP 248-253 library classification to cater the demands of ever growing multifaceted and multidimensional micro subjects. With the result there has been a gradual change in the enumerative pattern of Dewey Decimal classification. Following main features of editions 18 to 21 vividly indicate that the Scheme is gradually becoming a faceted classification scheme. However, Add Device is the wonder device the extensive use of which has added synthetic element in the *Scheme.*

Edition 18 (1971). (i) The two volume pattern was changed into three volume pattern - Volume 1. Introduction, Table, Volume 2. Schedules and Volume 3. Relative Index; (ii) The auxiliary tables were increased to 7, which was an indicator of its inclination to become more faceted and to increase its capacity to provide co-extensive class number; (iii) The Divide Like Device was named as Add Device; (iv) The index was so designed that it provided an entry for every significant term enumerated in the Schedules and Tables.

Edition 19 (1979). (i) DDC for the first time was published by computerised photo composition; (ii) In Table 1. Standard Subdivisions Table of precedence was added, the notation- 08 used for Collection up to Edition 18 was used for History and description of the subject among groups of persons. (iv) In Areas Table 2, notations 41 -42 were revised to conform to the reorganised local administrative pattern of the United Kingdom; (v) A supplementary Table 3-A was added to Table 3; (vi) The main class Sociology was extended from 301 to 301-307 making use of class numbers 302-307 which were left unused for last twenty years. Later in 1982, a more detailed version of 301-307 sociology was published separately in the form of a booklet; (vii) The class numbers 324 and 329 used for Electoral Process and Political Parties respectively were recasted in 324 The Political Process.

Edition 20 (1989). (i) On July 29, 1988 , Forest Press and Dewey Decimal Classification became a part of the OCLC - Online Computer Library Centre, Ohio, which published the Scheme in four volumes :- V1 - Introduction. Table, Volume 2 and Volume 3-Schedules, Volume 4. Relative Index. Manual; (ii) The Scheme was for the first time produced by an online Editorial Support System (ESS), which eliminated the manual work in editing the

DDC, (iii) In Table 1 *Add Tables* were provided under notation -0909 and - 093 - 099; (iv) In Areas Table 2 notation - 711 British Columbia was completely revised; (v) Table 3 was subdivided into three sub-tables:- 3-A, 3-B and 3-C; (vi) A new table termed as Equivalence Table was added in Volume 1 to provide a vivid picture of the class numbers used in old and new editions for similar subjects in completely revised main classes; (vii) The three summaries were shifted from Volume 1 to Volume 2; (viii) A completely revised schedule for 780 Music was incorporated. (ix) The class numbers 001-006 were extensively revised and 004-006 assigned to newly evolved subjects - Data Processing and Computer Science; (x) Multiple summaries were introduced in 6 main classes and also in Areas Table in notation -7 North America; (xi) Relative Index was trimmed from pages 1218 to 730 pages by weeding out unnecessary entries and (xii) Manual on the use of DDC was incorporated in Volume 4. In Edition 19, the Manual was published as a separate Volume.

Edition 21 (1996): (i) This edition has been revised using the 'Policy of to keep pace with knowledge'. (ii) Christian bias has been reduced. (iii) Completely revised schedules have been provided for 350-354 Public administration, 370 Education 560-590 Life Sciences, 296 Judaism, 297 Islam and 368 Insurance. (iv) Facet indicators and notational synthesis are basic elements in the design of two completely revised schedules 350 - 354 and 560 -590. (v) The term phoenix schedule has been replaced by completely revised schedule. (vi) Manual has been expanded. (vii) The terminology used in the scheme has been updated to achieve currency and reflect international usage. (viii) Edition 21 is the first edition prepared with online access to the OCLC online union catalogue for guidance on literary warrant, (ix) It is published in four volumes.

With all these additions and modifications there is no change in the number building procedure of DDC. However, the increased use of Add Device has widened the scope for providing an exact and specific class number to a subject.

EDITIONS 19 AND 20 - MAIN FEATURES

The following vivid description would help the classifier in understanding the dynamics and practical applicability of both the editions of DDC.

1. The three volumes of Edition 19 have been bifurcated into four volumes in Edition 20. The information distributed in these volumes is as follows:-

Volume	Edition 19	Edition 20
Volume 1	Introduction, Editor' Introduction, Tables, Relocations and Reductions, List of changed numbers, Summaries	New Features in Edition 20, Introduction to DDC, Tables, Relocations and Reductions, Comparative Tables Equivalence Tables Summaries (shifted to Vol. 2)
Volume 2	Schedules	Volume 2. Summaries, Schedules - 000 - 500
Volume 3	Volume 3 - Relative Index.	Volume 3 - Schedules 600 - 900
		Volume 4. Relative Index, Manual

INTRODUCTION

The Introductory part describes the main characteristics, the basic plan and how to classify documents using DDC. It is a useful guide for the classifier as it defines, explains and describes the rules and procedure for selecting class number, use of Tables and Index. In Edition 20 the Introduction has been completely rewritten making it easier and more systematic for understanding DDC.

TABLES

The seven tables provide notations that are added to class numbers enumerated in the Schedules. The notations of these tables may be added using Add Device where the instructions for its use is given and also through Table I-Standard Subdivisions.

EQUIVALENCE TABLES

In Edition 20, a new Table designated as Equivalence Table

has been added in Volume 1. The basic function of this Table is to provide a vivid picture of the numbers used for similar subjects in old and new editions when a Schedule has been completely revised like 780 Music and -711 British Columbia in Edition 20. In the Equivalence Table the numbers are provided in the following manner:

Table A

Edition 19	Edition 20	Notes
781.7	781.62	Folk music
784.9	783	

Table B

Edition 20	Edition 19	Notes
781.62	781.7	
783	784.9	The Voice

SUMMARIES

There are two types of summaries in Edition 19. In Edition 20 these have been increased to three types.

1. SUMMARIES OF THE SCHEDULES

The three Summaries which till Edition 19 were part of volume I have been shifted to Volume 2 in Edition 20. The main function of these summaries is to help the classifier in understanding the way the Universe of knowledge is divided in the Schedules. The First Summary enumerates the 10 Main Divisions, the Second divides these 10 divisions into 100 divisions and the 1000 divisions of the Third Summary provide a vivid picture of the main divisions and subdivisions with three digited numbers, which helps in understanding the structure and scope of the various Main Classes of DDC.

2. SINGLE - LEVEL SUMMARIES IN SCHEDULES AND TABLES

The single-level summaries are also available both in Editions 19 and 20. This type of summaries provides a glimpse of the subdivisions in which a specific main division is subdivided both in Schedules and Tables e.g.:

133.1	Apparitions
.3	Divinatory arts
.4	Demonology and witchcraft
.5	Astrology
.6	Palmistry
.7	Psychic phenomenon
.9	Spiritualism.

3. MULTI-LEVEL SUMMARIES IN THE SCHEDULES AND TABLES

In Edition 20 the introduction of multi-level summaries both in schedules and Tables has added one more feather in the scheme. These multi-level summaries take over the charges from the third summary. Where the work of third summary ends the work of multi-level summaries begin as these provide a complete overview of those classes that have sub-divisions extending for more than two pages. For example 340 Law. The multi-level summary for Law on pages 394-395 (Volume 2) enumerates the subdivisions of classes beginning with 340 upto 348. The classifier, thereby, has a clear picture how different classes of Law are subdivided and type of subjects enumerated under them. However, Edition 20 has provided multi-level summaries only for eight major divisions like 330 Economics, 340 Law, 350 Public Administration, 370 Education, 610 Medical Sciences, 620 Engineering, 780 Music and in Areas for - 4 Europe and - 7 North America. May be in future, these multi-level summaries are provided in the beginning of each main class to facilitate the classifier to have an overview of the main class and a direct linkage from third summary to multi-level summary to make it more easier to understand as to how knowledge is divided in DDC.

SCHEDULES

In Edition 19, only Volume 2 was designated as Schedules, whereas in Edition 20 Volumes 2 and 3 are designated as Schedules. These include the following:

Volume 2:	Summaries and Schedules 000-599.
Volume 3:	Schedules 600-999.

The Schedules form the bedrock of DDC system in which the Universe of knowledge is divided in main classes, main divisions and subdivisions. The classifier is, therefore, required to acquaint himself with the Schedules in the following manner:

1. the ten main classes in which the whole universe of knowledge is divided - *See* the First Summary provided at the end of Volume 1 (Ed. 19) and in the beginning of Volume 2 (Ed. 20)
2. the main divisions of each main class - *See* Second Summary.
3. the main divisions of each main division - *See* Third Summary.
4. then see the subdivisions provided in single-level summaries in the Schedules. For this select one main class and make yourself conversant with the method used for subdividing classes in different disciplines and subjects.
5. this step is the most important as the classifier is required to see under each class number the followings:

5a. the instruction to 'Use Standard subdivisions 01 - 09' from Table 1.

5b. the various notes which provide useful information with regard to the class number under which this note is given, e.g.: class here comprehensive works on ...or class here...or including...etc.

5c. the way Add Device is used to add numbers from Schedules and Tables.

5d. the options which permit the classifier to use other than Standard numbers to meet the specific needs of the library.

5e. the footnote instructions.

5f. the Special Tables - in classes for which these Tables are provided.

5g. the use of Precedence Tables - in subjects where these are provided.

5h. the citation and precedence order to decide when a subject indicates multiple aspects or characteristics.

6. The notations:

6a. DDC class number is not less than three digisted. To make it three digited one or two zeros may be added after the significant digit.

6b. a dot is used after the third digit. DDC in its instruction uses the term 'decimal point for this dot. However, it has been made clear in its glossary that the 'Decimal point is the dot that follows the third digit in a DDC number. In strict usage the word 'decimal' is not accurate'.

RELATIVE INDEX AND MANUAL

RELATIVE INDEX

Relative Index is primarily a glossary of terms used in the Schedules and Tables. It is named Relative Index as it relates subjects to disciplines. In the Schedules of DDC different aspects of a subject are enumerated under different disciplines in accordance to their relation to them. In the Index all these different aspects are brought together under the specific name of the subject which also indicate their locations vide their artificial name in ordinal numbers assigned to them in the Schedules.

FORMAT AND USE OF THE RELATIVE INDEX

The Relative Index of DDC is an alphabetical list of subjects enumerated in the Schedules and Tables. The Index entries are arranged alphabetical word by word. For example:

Botanical Sciences

Botanists

Botany

Botetourt Co. Va

The different aspects of a subject which are scattered throughout the Schedules under different disciplines are grouped together in one place under the name of that specific subject. The name of the specific subject is inlisted as Main Heading, the first letter of its name always being the capital letter, the entries under it are arranged using small letter, except in case of proper names. This also provides a vivid picture of coordinate and subordinate relations of the subjects. For example:-

Edition 20	**Edition 19**
Gems 553.8	Gems 553.8
carving 736.2	eco. geol 553.8
economic giology 553.8	eng. materials 620.198
jewelry 739.27	foundation 624.153 8
material science 620.198	structure 624.189 89
mining 622.38	s.a.other spec - uses
	mining
prospecting 622.188	soc & eco aspects see
synthetic 666.88	Primary Industries
	technology 622.38
	prospecting 622.188
	synthetic
	manufacturing *see*
	Secondary Industries
	technology 666.88

The Index contains an entry for every significant name including synonyms and selected terms in common use. For example: (Ed. 20)

Chromium	669.734
chemical engineering	661.0532
chemistry	546.532
decorative arts	739.58
economic geology	553.464 3
material science	620.189 34
metallography	669.957 34
metallurgy	673.734
mining	622.346 43
organic chemistry	547.055 32

Cross Reference Device is yet another method in the Relative Index to provide information regarding those aspects of a subject which are classed under a broad heading, it may refer to a synonym or to a related term or a subject classed as a component part of the subject located elsewhere. In Edition 19 different types of cross references are used in the Index e.g. *see; other relations see; other aspects see; see also* etc. whereas in Edition 20, *see also* references only are being used. The elimination of unlikely entries and removal of *see references* has improved the format and reduced the size of the Index. It is now much easier to use the Relative Index. For example:-

Edition 19

Performance
  acting *see* Acting
    dramatic performances
  contracting
  education 371.5
  s. a. *specific* levels of education
  s. a. *other* special subjects
evaluation
  executive management 658.4013
rating
  employees *see* Evaluation of
    employees
standards metrology 389.63
  misc. aspects *see*
    standardisation metrology
  production management *see*
    quality control production
    management.

Edition 20

Performance Art 700
  fine arts 702.81
Performance cont-
  racting education 371.15
Performance evaluation
  computer science 004.029 7
  engineering 621.390297
Performance rating
  personal management
  executive 658.312 5
  management 658.401 3
  pub. administration 350.142
  cent. govt. 352.005 14
Performance scores 780
  treatise 780.264
Performance standards
  commerce 389.63
  production management
    658.562

The following abbreviations have been used to indicate different Tables :-

		Edition 19	Edition 20
1.	Standard Subdivisions	s.s.	T1
2.	Areas	areas	T2
3.	Subdivisions of Individual Literature	lit. sub	T3
4.	Subdivisions of Individual Languages	lang. sub	T4
5.	Racial, Ethnic, National Groups	r. e. n.	T5
6.	Languages	lang.	T6
7.	Persons	pers.	T7

The classifier should also note that if a term is enumerated in the Tables, then the notation is always preceded by a dash together with specific name of the Table. For example :-

	Edition 19	**Edition 20**
Formulas	ss - 0122	T1 - 0122
Foster Children	pers. - 0441	T7 - 0441
France	areas - 44	T2 - 44

Interdisciplinary Numbers are not provided in the Index (i) when the unintended term is ambiguous e.g.:

Liquid Phases
liquid - state physics 530.424

(ii) When the interdisciplinary subject might be misleading e.g.:

Poodle
animal husbandry 636.72
see also dogs.

(ii) When unintended term has no disciplinary focus.

Although the Relative Index includes most of the terms enumerated in the Schedules and Tables, but it is not exhaustive therefore:-

(i) If the term sought is not found, the classifier should try under a synonym or under another term of the same root or under a related term or under a broader term or consult the Schedules and Tables directly.

(ii) The classifier should never assign class numbers to documents solely on the basis of Relative Index, as he/she might miss helpful guidance that is provided in the Schedules e.g. add instructions, options and various other notes.

(iii) In all cases, the discipline and its class number must be checked and verified from the Schedules *or* Tables, where complete information about the class number, what it includes and its correct use can be found.

THE MANUAL

The most important feature of Edition 20 is making the Manual as part of Volume 4. The Manual was first published in 1982 as separate publication entitled 'Manual on the use of the Dewey Decimal Classification Edition 19'. The Manual describes the policies and practices of the Decimal Classification Division of the Library of Congress. The Manual assists the classifier in the application of DDC Schedules and Tables, offers advice on classing in difficult areas and explains how to choose between related terms.

II

BASIC PLAN AND STRUCTURE

Dewey Decimal Classification is basically a Enumerative Classification Scheme in which the Universe of knowledge is organised by traditional academic disciplines or field of study and *not* by subjects. It means that a specific subject may be enumerated under different disciplines from the point of its relation to that particular discipline. For example, the subject *Copper* may be classified under Arts, Natural Sciences or Applied Sciences. It is therefore, imperative for the classifier that before assigning DDC class number to a document the thought content must be studied to know its real discipline. However, Relative Index is a wonderful *Guide* which indicates clearly the coorelation of a subject to different disciplines.

The *Principle of Hierarchy* With *Principle of Decimal Fraction* is used to divide the universe of knowledge. Therefore, the Hierarchy is clearly seen both in its structure and notation. The structural hierarchy is expressed by first dividing the universe of knowledge into Ten Main classes 0-9 (As is given in First Summary), each main class is further subdivided into ten divisions (As is given in Second Summary) and each division into ten sections (As is given in Third Summary), each section again is divided into ten sub sections. This hierarchical pattern of DDC is simultaneously depicted through the length of notation used for each class. The degree of specificity of a class is usually indicated by the length of notation and the corresponding depth of indention of the heading to denote these divisions and sections. The generic term *class* is used to denote them. The Indo-Arabic numerals 0-9 are used to divide the universe of knowledge in the following manner:

0.0 Generalities

0.1 Philosophy and Psychology

0.2 Religion

0.3 Social Sciences

0.4 Languages

0.5 Natural Sciences and mathematics

0.6 Technology (Applied Sciences)

0.7 The arts Fine and decorative Arts

0.8 Literature (Belles - letters) and rhetoric

0.9 Geography, history and auxiliary disciplines.

However, the DDC class number is not less than three digited. To make it three digited one or two zeros are to be added after every significant digit used to denote a class. It means the zero or zeros added after a significant digit have no semantic value. For example : 1 Philosophy is to be assigned class number 100, 2 Religion 200 and so on. The first zero and the decimal point are taken as implied and the class numbers are simply written 100, 200, 300 and not 0.100, 0.300 etc.

Each main class is further subdivided into ten divisions. The third digit in each three digited class number indicate the section. For example, the class number 63*0* is used for General works on agriculture, 63*1* for specific technique, 632 for plant diseases, 63*3* for field Crops, 63*5* for Garden Crops, 63*7* for Dairy, and 63*8* for Insect culture.

The three digited class numbers are further subdivided using Indo - Arabic numerals 0-9. As per general rule after every third digit a decimal point (dot) is to be used. However, in practice the decimal point is used only after the first block of three digited class number, thereafter vacant space is left in place of dot. For example; 637.708 9 Dog anatomy.

ASSIGNING THE CLASS NUMBERS

Before classifying a document and assigning class number to it, the classifier is required to analyse the thought content of the document, to know the exact discipline and then the exact subject. Once the subject is determined the classifier may take help of the three summaries or the Relative Index to know its class number. But it is imperative that the class number is assigned to a document only on the basis of the Schedules. As Schedules are the only source wherein the information relating to Add note, order of precedence, various types of notes are given. It is therefore, necessary that the classifier should make himself fully conversant with the anatomy of the Schedules. For this purpose the step wise guidelines are provided in chapter I of this book under the heading Schedules.

NOTES

In DDC Notes form an integral part of the process used for selecting or deciding the class numbers of a document. Before finalising the class number, it is obligatory on the part of the classifier that he carefully goes through the notes, if any, given under that particular class number. These notes may be categorised in the following manner:-

A. Notes That Describe What Is Found In A Class

A1. Definition and Scope notes: This type of notes help the classifier in two ways : (i) by providing a simple and formal definition of a subject, as is given under 020 Library and Information Science; (ii) it indicates the other areas which are included in that particular class, which helps the classifier in understanding the scope of the class. For example :-

320.512 Traditional Liberalism

Ideologies and theories stressing rationalism...

A2. Former Heading notes: Such notes are given if the nomenclature of the heading used for a class in the previous edition has been changed, without any change in its meaning. For example :-

324.65 Voting procedures

Former heading : Polling

A3. Variant name notes: Notes which inform the classifier the other synonyms or near synonyms terms. For example :-

330.157 Marginal Utility Schools

Variant names : neo-classical, Austrian school

A4. Class - here notes: This type of notes inform the classifier that all those areas or subjects - broader or narrower, which are enumerated under that particular class where this note is given, should be allotted the same class number which is used for that class. For example :-

510 Mathematics

Class - here : Finite mathematics

- 544 Rajasthan

Class - here : Thar (Indian) Desert

B Notes That Specify Subjects In Waiting

This type of notes are used invariably in each and every edition and to some extent in every main class. Subjects which have little literary warrant, but may became a subject of importance in future, *or* subjects on which DDC editorial board has not decided where to place it permanently, *or* the term used for the heading is a technical term *or* the subject includes other subjects as well. These clubbed classes may or may not get a specific class number in future edition. The terms used for such notes are:-

Example, Including, contains, common name etc. For example:-

B1. Example note:

302.14 Social participation

Example :- cooperation voluntarism

B2. Including note:

302 Social interaction

Including Social perception, social choice, attraction, influence, cooperation and competition (Ed. 19)

Some of these get specific class number in Ed. 20. For example

302.13 Social choice

Including attraction, influence.

B3. Contains notes list: All the major component of the class, till these do not have their own subdivisions.

For example :

583.976 Fagales

Contains Fagaceae (oak family), corylaceae

B4. **Common name notes:** This type of notes are used mainly in the Main Class Biology wherein it is necessary to inform about the other common names used for a particular plant.

WARNING

However, the classifier has been instructed not to use either Standard subdivisions or any other number building techniques with classes identified by these notes.

C. **Notes That Make Classifier Aware of Related Subjects or Topics:**

This type of notes are in general used when the DDC editorial board is not clear about the placing of a particular class or when classifier is required to see another related class to become very sure about, the correct classing of a subject.

C1. **Class elsewhere notes:** This type of notes instruct the classifier that a subject-broader or narrower, needs to be classed elsewhere and not under that class wherein the note is given. For example:-

305.52 Upper classes (Ed. 19)

.55 Middle classes (Bourgeois)

Class wealthy, middle classes, intellectual *elites* in 305.52

C2. **Class here note:** This type of note instructs to class the specified subject or concept in that class number itself. For example:-

305.52 Upper classes (Ed. 20)

.55 Middle classes (Bourgeois)

.555 Intelligentsia

Class here *intellectual elites.*

Both these examples make it very clear that the DDC policy changes in every edition relating to subjects identified by different types of notes and creates problems for the classifier.

Class - here note is also used to make provision for concepts that overlap the heading. For example :-

-54 India

Class here Himalayas

-78 Western United States

Class here Rocky Mountains

C3. **Cross References:** Cross references are special kind of notes which direct the classifier (i) to *see* class number for a given subject enumerated elsewhere in the schedules. For example:

351 Central Government

For specific Central Government *see* 353-354.

541.22 Molecular structure

For quantum chemistry *see* 541.28

(ii) *See also references*: refer to subjects which are clearly and in real sense related to the class wherein such note is given. For example :-

641.22 Wine

Class here grape wine

see also 641.23 for sake (ricewine)

D. Notes Informing Changes In the Schedules and Tables:

Every new edition of DDC tries to compete with the growing Universe of Subjects through complete Revision, Relocations and Expansions. It becomes, therefore obligatory to inform the classifier about these changes and modifications. Information regarding complete Revision generally is given under the heading 'New Features In Edition...' in the Intorductory Part of the New Edition. Whereas the changes and modifications made in the Schedules and Tables are notified, through the terms - Revision, Discontinued, and Relocation.

D1. **Revision notes** : In DDC four types of rivisions are invariably used while revising a Edition. These are:-

(i) *Routine revision*: which is limited to updating terminology, clarifying notes, and providing modest expansions;

(ii) *Substantial revision*: revisions made in a class that requires major redifinitions and significant relocations;

(iii) *Extensive revision*: in which a Schedule or Table is revised thoroughly. The outcome of which is that only outlines of the old Schedule remains intact; and

(iv) *Complete Revision*: upto Ed. 19 it was termed as Phoenix Schedule. The Schedule or Table is so revised that only the *Base Number* of the class remains as in the previous edition. For first three types of rivisions the changes are indicated through Revision notes.

D2. **Discontinued notes :** When certain provisions of previous edition become redundant due to various reasons– such as topics which no more represent current literature or represent a distinction which is no longer valid in the literature or subject is classed in another number, then class numbers representing such classes are indicated through Discontinued number notes.

D3. **Relocation notes :** Relocations are used in DDC to make adjustments in the schedules, for accommodating new subjects and to adjust a subject the meaning of which has undergone a change. Accordingly the shifting and shunting of subjects from one number to another in successive editions are indicated through relocation notes. Relocations are used to-

(i) to eliminate dual provisions;

(ii) to regularise the use of standard subdivisions;

(iii) to provide uniformity of development for parallel subjects;

(iv) to ensure proper subject relationship and;

(v) to rectify erroneous placement of subjects.

Relocation may be either total or partial. In case of total relocation, the entire class number used in previous edition is vacated. Whereas in case of partial relocation, only few numbers may be changed, in that case the class number is enclosed in square brackets with the term *formerly*. For example :-

301[0.19] Psychological principle

Relocated in 302.

362.71 Direct relief

Protection for abused and neglected children relocated to 362.768

362.298 Cocaine [formerly 362.293]

OPTIONS

At a number of places in the Schedules and Tables the classifier has been allowed through *options* to use other than standard numbers to comply the local needs of the library. These options allow the classifier to use some specific symbol or letter or number, etc. The following example makes this more clear:

050 General serial publications and their indexes

051-059 In specific languages and language families

By language in which originally written

(*Option A*: To give local emphasis and a shorter number to serial publications in a specific language, place them first by use of a letter or another symbol e.g. Hindi language serial publications 05H (Preceding 051).

(*Option B*: arrange serial publications alphabetically under 050).

(*Option C*: To give local emphasis and a shorter number to serial publications in a specific language other than English, class them in this number [i.e. in 051 allotted to American]. In that case class American English language serial publications in 052).

059 In other languages

Add to base number 059 notation 7-9 from Table 6.

It means that the Indian libraries have 3 options besides the Standard number 059 to classify Hindi language serial publications.

Such options are also provided to give preferred treatment to specific jurisdiction or areas, as in Main class 340 Law, or to a specific language as in Main classes 400 Languages and 800 Literature or classes where two areas are to be used together as in 327.3-.9 Foreign relations of specific nations.

In DDC there are innumerable subjects both in Schedules

and Tables which are allocated to two different class numbers. In such cases both preferred and optional numbers are indicated, e.g.

-385	Attica
	(Option: Class Attica, Marathon in -4951, Athens in -49512)
-49512	Athens
	(Option: Class here ancient Athens; prefer - 385)
224[.37]	Baruch
	(Use of this number is optional prefer 229.5)
229.5	Baruch...
	(Option: Class Baruch in 224.37...)

In Edition 20 both optional number as well as directions regarding use of options are provided in parentheses whereas in Edition 19 only optional numbers are kept in square brackets and not the directions to use options.

For example:-

828		English miscellaneous writings
(*Ed. 19*)	[.99]	English language literatures....
(*Ed. 20*)	(.99)	English language literatures...

However, no such symbols - parentheses or square-brackets are used either in Edition 19 or 20 for options permitting alphabetical or chronological arrangements.

Example:-

Ed. 19

001.6424 Program language and coding

Subarrange by name of program language

e.g. FORTRAN 001.6424F6

Ed. 20

005.133 Specific programming language

Arrange alphabetically by name of programming language

e.g. COBOL.

ADD DEVICE

Add Device is the most important method used in DDC to subdivide or individualise a subject. The gradual increase in the use of Add Device in every new edition of DDC has simultaneous impact on its enumerative nature, that is making it more and more faceted. In Edition 20, there are innumerable classes wherein the enumerated classes of Edition 19 have been replaced by Add Device.

Add Device which was termed as Divide like device up to Edition 17 is used to add numbers from the Schedules and Tables.

Add Device in Schedules

There are class numbers in DDC which are to be subdivided by the classifier by adding to them the numbers enumerated elsewhere in the Schedules. In other words, it means subdividing a subject on the basis of the subjects already enumerated in DDC. This method to some extent is analogous to the 'Subject Device' of Colon Classification.

The language used in the instructions of Add Device is as follows:

Ed. 19

1. Add 001-999 to base number...
2. Add to base number...the numbers following...in..

Ed. 20

1. Add to base number....notation 001-999
2. Add to base number...the number following ... in...

There is minor difference in the language of first instruction in the Editions 19 and 20. However, the language of Edition 20 will be used in all practical examples of this book.

MEANING OF THE TERMS USED IN ABOVE INSTRUCTIONS

Base number

Base number is the class number of that specific subject which is to be further subdivided by the classifier. The add instruction, therefore, specifically indicates that the numbers enumerated elsewhere are to be added only after this Base number, e.g.:

266 Missions

266.1-.9 Of specific denominations and sects

Add to base number 266 the numbers following 28 in 281-289

Here the Add instructions is under 266.1-.9 but the number used as base number is 266, and only after this base number the numbers enumerated from 281 to 289 are to be added.

As the base number is mentioned specifically where Add Device is to be used there is as such no problem for the classifier to know the specific class number which is to be further subdivided.

Numbers following

The notation indicated by 'numbers following' is that number which is not to be used while adding its subdivisions to 'base number'. It means it is a class number whose succeeding numbers only are to be added to the base number, e.g.:

266.1-.9 Of specific denominations...

Add to base number 266 the numbers following 28 to 281-289

Here the class number 28 is indicated by the term 'numbers following' i.e. numbers coming after 28 only are to be added and not 28. So, on the basis of the above instruction we may add to base number 266 the following numbers.

284.5	Huguenot churches
284.6	Moravian churches
289.1	Universalist church

Add numbers following to base number 266

[28]4.5*	266	266.45
[28]4.6	266	266.46
[28]9.1	266	266.91

* Square brackets are used in all the examples to indicate the 'numbers following,' i.e. numbers which are not to be added.

PRACTICAL APPLICATION

1. Add to base number...notation 001-999

Through this instruction the classifier is permitted to add any number from the Schedules which starts *with 001* knowledge and ends *with 999* extraterrestrial worlds. Hence the required notation from the Schedules may be added directly to base number where this instruction is given.

Examples:

Add to Base No 343.078 notation 001 - 999

Analysis: Herein the classifier is permitted to add to base number 343.078 any class number from the schedules.

Base No.		**Agriculture - 630**	
343.078	+	63[0]	= 344.07863
343.078	+	**Mines** - 622	= 344.078622

1. Title: Library classification of Social Sciences

025.46 Classification of specific subjects...

Add to base number 025.46 notation 001-999

Base No.		**Social Sciences**
025.46	+	3[00]

C. No. 025.463

2. Title: Classification of Choreography

Base No.		**Choreography**
025.46	+	782.82

C. No 025.4678282

3. Title: Aptitude test in mathematics

153.94 Aptitude tests

.94001 - .94999 Tests for aptitude in specific fields

Add to base number 153.94 notation 001-999

510 Mathematics

Base No.		**Mathematics**
153.94	+	51[0]

C. No. 153.9451

Note: If the class number ends with zero or zeros, then these are not to be added as these zeros do not have any significance and are added only to make the notations of DDC three digited.

2. To Add Subdivisions of a Main Class

Add Device is also used to permit the classifier to add subdivisions of a main class, discipline or subject to individualise or subdivide a class.

In this category of Add Device, the classifier is required to note carefully the language of the instruction through which he is permitted what to add and from where. The language of the instruction may be as follows:

(i) Add to base number 630.2 the numbers following 5 in 510-590.

Analysis: Herein the classifier is permitted to add to base number 630.2 all the subdivision from 510-590.

For example:

630	Agriculture and related Technologies
630.2	Scientific Principles
Base No.	**General Principles (Mathematics)**
630.2	[5]11
C. No. 630.211	Use of mathematical principles in Agriculture.

(ii) Add to base number 926 the numbers following 6 in 610 - 690.

Analysis : Here in the classifier is permitted to add subdivisions from the Main class 610-690 - Applied Sciences

920	Biography	
926	Persons in technology	
Base No.	**Medical Sciences**	
926	+	[6] 1 [0]
C. No. 926.1	Biography of doctors	

(iii) Add to base number 338.13 the numbers following 63 in 633 - 638.

Analysis: In this instruction the classifier is instructed to add numbers of one specific discipline 63 Agriculture and related technologies only. e.g.:

338	Production
338.1	Agriculture
.13	Financial aspects. Price

Base No.		**Rice**
(i) 338.13	+	[63]3.18

C. No. 338.13318 Price of rice

(ii) 338.13 + [63]7.3 Cheese Production

C. No. 338.1373 Prices of cheese Productions

(iv) In the numbers following process the digits that is the digits which are not be added may increase up to the last subdivision of a class number. e.g.:

Add to base number 629.1331 the numbers following 629.133 in 629.1332 to 629.1333

629.1	Aerospace Engineering
.133	Aircraft types
.1331	Model

Base No.		**Airships**		**Model of Airships**
629.1331	+	[629.133]24	=	629.133124
		Rocket Planes		**Model of Rocket Planes**
629.1331	+	[629.133]38	=	629.133138
		Sea planes		**Model of Sea planes**
629.1331	+	[629.133]347	=	629.1331347

Add Device and Special Tables

The Special Tables which are designend to meet the specific needs of specific subjects also take help of Add Device. However, the permission to add notation of special table is restricted through footnote instructions which are indicated through symbols like *(asterisk) or †(daggers). The procedure to add notation from special table is described in Chapter X of this book.

Add Device and Tables

Add Device is also used to add notation from Table 2-7 of Volume 1. Wherever in the Schedules the instruction to add notation from Tables is given, the name or number of Table is always indicated in the instruction e.g. Add "Areas" notation 1-9 from Table 2 to base number 027.0 (Ed. 19) Add to base number 027.0 notation 1-9 from Table 2 (Ed. 20).

Title: Libraries in Rajasthan

Base No.	**Areas Table 2**
027.0	-544

C. No. 027.0544

Note: The classifier is required to add complete number from the Table directly to the base bumber as indicated in the instruction. The classifier is not supposed to delete or omit any digit from the notations of the Table before adding the notaion to the base number.

CLASSIFYING A COMPLEX SUBJECT

Being an Eumerative Classification DDC does not provide general methods or devices to classify documents which deal with more than one subject or discipline. Add Device is the only device which to some extent may help in providing class numbers to such subjects, but its use is restricted by the Editorial Board of DDC, which decides in which classes the instructions for Add Device should be given. Keeping in view this shortcoming the Editor in his Introduction has provided following guidelines for classifying complex subjects.

More Than One Subject

(A) Class a Work dealing with interrelated subjects with the subject that is being acted upon. For instance, class an analytical work dealing with Shakespeare's influence on keats with keats.

(B) Class a work on two subjects with the subject recieving fuller treatment.

(C) If two subjects recieve equal treatment, and are not used to introduce or explain one another, class the work with the subject whose number comes first in DDC Schedules.

However, if there are specific notes, instruction on citation order or precedence order, then only these are to be followed. This rule should also be disregarded when the two topics are two major subdivision of a subject. The broad class number only should be allotted to such document.

(D) Class a Work on three or more subjects that are all subdivisions of a broader subject in the first higher number that includes them all.

(E) Subdivisions beginning with zero should be avoided if there is a choice between 0 and 1-9 at the same point in the hierarchy of the notation.

Similarly, subdivisions beginning with 00 should be avoided when there is a choice between 00 and 0.

More Than One Discipline

If the subject of a document deals with two or more disciplines and indicates two or more points of view or aspects, than it should be classed in the following manner:-

(A) Use the ready made class number given for an interdisciplinary work in the Schedules or Relative Index. However, it also must be seen that this number contains significant material on the discipline to which it is related.

(B) If the interdisciplinary number is not given, then class in the discipline that gives the subject fullest treatment;

(C) When classifying interdisciplinary works, possibilities of its classing in the main class 000 Generalities must also be explored;

(D) If any of these is not applicable then guidelines given for *More Than One Subject* may be followed.

CITATION ORDER AND ORDER OF PRECEDENCE

The main function of the Citation order and Order of Precedence is to help the classifier in classifying a document the thought content of which deals with more than one characteristics.

CITATION ORDER

The Citation Order has been defined by DDC in its glossary as 'the order in which the facets or characteristics of a class are to be combined in number building'. DDC being an enumerative classification scheme does not provide the autonomy to the classifier to classify a document with multiple facets on the basis of analysis and synthesis nor it provides a fixed formula to combine at least two areas. It is only on the sheer good will of the DDC Editorial Board where to allow the classifier to build or synthesise a number using two or more aspects or characteristics. As and where Board feels necessary the specific instruction is given which specify what should be the sequence of the characteristics and how these are to be combined. The Citation order is therefore, a ruling of the Board how and where to combine different facets of a complex subject. However, the Citation order instruction is in general used to combine two areas *or* areas and historical periods and in exceptional cases such as in Law to combine enumerated subjects. For example, in Main Class 340 Law, under different Branches of Law under the heading specific jurisdiction and areas the instruction to add first notations from Table 2 and then subdivisions of that branch is given. According to which the Citation order should be:

Law	**+**	**Branch of Law (Constitutional Law)**	**+**	**Jurisdiction (India)**	**+**
34	+	2	+	54	+

Subdivision as under 342	**+**	**Standard Subdivisions**
342.07	+	0264

C. No. 342.54070264 Court decisions relating to Indian election law.

This number building instruction therefore, defines the limits of the class number to be provided to a complex subject. For example the number building instruction may allow to add two areas or area and historical period only after which the class number can not be extended further. Many such examples are available in Chapter III Table 1. Standard Subdivisions of this book.

ORDER OF PRECEDENCE/TABLE OF PRECEDENCE

DDC also provides clear directions to the classifier through order of precedence note or table of precedence, which one of the two or more numbers is to be chosen, when the numbers represent different characteristics of a subject and more so when these cannot be shown in full by number building. A clear example of Citation order and Order of Precedence is available in Table 5*.

The Tables of Precedence are of two types - *one* which directs to observe strictly the order as provided in table of precedence, e.g.:

Table of Precedence under:

351.848 Services to other groups

and *second* which directs to verify if other instructions are provided for the same before following the order of the table of precedence. The instruction states: 'Unless other instructions are given, observe the following table of precedence'. Such tables are available under 155, 351.84, 352, etc.

PRECEDENCE NOTE

The role of the precedence note is to indicate which characteristic is to be selected for works covering more than one characteristic. The note generally reads as follows:

'Unless other instructions are given, class complex subjects with aspects in two or more subdivisions of this schedule in the number *coming first in schedule*' e.g. as under 331.3-331.6 or '*coming last in the schedule as*' e.g. as under 351.83 or 629.04.

SYMBOLS

There are some distinct symbols used in DDC which are used to perform different roles in the use of enumerated numbers in the Schedules and Tables. These are as follows:

[ ] *Square brackets*: The number kept within square brackets connotes following different meanings:

(a) **Number discontinued:** The direction 'Number discontinued class in...Do not use; class in...or relocated to, etc., is provided under all those bracketed numbers, wherein new number

* See Chapter VIII of this book.

has been allotted to the subject for which this bracketed number was used in previous edition. Therefore, in place of this bracketed number, classifier is required to use the new number as indicated in the direction.

For example:

Ed. 19	Ed. 20	
301.72	301.[72]	Nonliterate Number discontinued; class in 301.7
394.2609	394.[2609]	Historical, geographical Do not use; class in 394.269
197.1	197[.1]	Finland Relocated to 198.8
321.5	321.[5]	Elitist systems Autocracy relocated to 321.6

(b) **Number used formerly:** In addition to the above procedure of indicating the new number under the bracketed number, this bracketed number is again repeated with the new number to make it more convenient for the classifier to know about the old number also and the term formerly is used for this which is also kept within brackets. For example:

Ed. 20

198.8 Finland [formerly 197.1]

Ed. 19

321.5 Elitist systems

Autocracies, theocracies...

Ed. 20

321.6 Absolute monarchy

Class here autocracy [formerly 321.5]

(c) **Never assigned or unassigned numbers:** There are also bracketed numbers against which the terms never assigned or unassigned is written. This indicates that such numbers are not in use in this edition but were in use in earlier editions. For example:

Ed. 19 and 20

[007] [Unassigned]

Most recently used in Edition 16

[008] [Never assigned]

(d) **Optional number:** In Edition 19 the number in square brackets is also used to indicate the optional numbers.

OTHER SYMBOLS

In DDC various enumerated subjects in the schedule are identified by symbols: *(asterisk) and † (dagger) which are used to direct the classifier to see the instructions given at the bottom of the same page and then add numbers to these identified class numbers accordingly. The footnote instructions are provided in the following manner:

*add to base number as instructed...

or

Add as instructed under.

or

(Optional number prefer...)

or

*Use 00 for standard subdivisions; see..

It is therefore obligatory for the classifier, to read the footnote instruction before using the identified class number for classifying the documents.

III

TABLE 1
STANDARD SUBDIVISIONS (SS)

Table 1 provides such subdivisions which are commonly applicable to all the classes enumerated in the Schedules from 001-999. In the classificatory terminology these are described as common subdivisions which may be added, as and when required, to the class numbers of specific disciplines, subjects or their subdivisions. According to DDC the 'subdivisions found in Table 1 that represent frequently recurring physical forms (dictionaries, periodicals) or approaches (history, research) applicable to any subject or discipline. These may be added to any number in the Schedules unless there are instructions to the contrary'.

Standard subdivisions were included in DDC Edition 2 and since then the Scheme has been using different names for these subdivisions in its different editions. The term Form Divisions was used upto Edition 12 and again in 15 and 16 editions. In Edition 13 the term Common subdivisions was used and in Edition 14 the term Uniform subdivisions. But from Edition 17 onwards the term Standard subdivisions is being used. It is only from Edition 17 that a separate Table is provided for Standard Subdivisions.

Kinds of Standard Subdivisions

The Manual of DDC Editions 19 and 20 describes the various kinds of Standard subdivisions enumerated in Table 1. These are :

1. Subdivisions which indicate Bibliographic Forms, such as encyclopaedias, periodicals, dictionaries, etc.
2. Subdivisions which in a restricted situation, may treat the whole subject, such as areas, historical periods and kinds of persons;
3. Subdivisions which bring the methods of other disciplines

to bear on the subject, e.g., management, education, scientific principles, etc.

4. Subdivisions which identify specific kinds of information about the subject, such as directories, product list, etc.
5. Subdivisions which relate the subject to its users such as the subject as a profession and work for a specific type of users.
6. Miscellaneous subdivisions such as biography.

STANDARD SUBDIVISIONS

GENERAL GUIDELINES

Before actual application of Standard subdivisions the classifier should know that:

1. the Standard subdivisions are never used alone but are added to the class numbers enumerated in the Schedules from 001 to 999;
2. that no official instruction is required for the use of Standard subdivisions, these may be added freely as and when required to class numbers of the specific subjects enumerated in the Schedules;
3. that preference should always be given to already enumerated Standard subdivisions class numbers in the Schedules;
4.. with the base digits of these already enumerated class numbers for standard subdivisions in the Schedules all other subdivisions enumerated in Table 1 may also be used e.g.:

    401 Philosophy and theory
    .2 classification
    .3 value
    .5 scientific principles

5. that the notation - 09 has two base digits - 091, 093 - 099 for Geographical isolates and - 0901 - 0909 for Historical isolates;
6. that there are certain subjects where in special or extended subdivisions for Standard Subdivisions are provided. For example, the notation -026 in Main class 340 Law for 342

- 347 or subdivisions as under 340.1 Theories of Law;

7. that there are subjects wherein special chronological subdivisions or Period Tables are provided. For example, Period Tables for 820 - 890 Literature of specific languages *or* chronological numbers enumerated under 722 - 724 Architectural Schools and 930 - 999 History of specific continents, countries ...,

8. that in DDC various types of notes or cross references indicate the correct SS number which should be used with a specific subject. For example

333	Land economics
.001	Philosophy and theory Class theories in 333.01
.0012	Classification Class land classification in 333. 73012
372	Elementary education
372 .01 -.08	Standard subdivisions
.[013]	Value
	Do not use class in 372.011
.[068]	Management
	Do not use class in 372.12

9. that the Standard subdivisions may be extended further on the basis of the subdivisions enumerated in the Schedules, e.g.

- 015	Scientific Principles
	Add to base number - 015 numbers
	following 5 in 510 -590

or using notations of other Tables, e.g.

- 024	Works for specific type of users
	Add to base number -024 notations
	- 03 - 099 from Table 7.

TABLE OF PRECEDENCE

The Table of Precedence is being provided in the beginning of Table 1 from Edition 19 onwards. The Table of Precedence enables the classifier to identify which Standard subdivision is to be used in case the specific subject indicates more than one Standard subdivisions. The direction provided in the Table states 'Unless other instructions are given, class works to which two or more standard subdivisions are applicable according to the following table of precedence'. The classifier is accordingly required:

1. to use only one SS if the specific subject indicates two or more SS,
2. that this one SS should be decided on the basis of the table of precedence.

USE OF MORE THAN ONE STANDARD SUBDIVISION - EXCEPTIONS

However, in DDC there are a few exceptions to this general rule, wherein SS may be used twice or more, e.g.:

1. **With -04 Special topics:** In Table 1 Standard Subdivisions -04 is allotted to Special topics of general applicability. The direction under -04 clearly states 'Use this subdivision only when it is specifically set forth in the Schedules. Add other Standard subdivisions -01-09 to it and its subdivisions as required'. In reality -04 is not a SS but is a type of device through which new development in a subject may be added. Therefore, the Standard subdivisions may be used with -04 as in case of other subjects enumerated in the Schedules, e.g.:

   Title: Teaching in community schools.
   372.10423 + -07(Table 1)
   C.No. 372.1042307

2. **When SS concept is displaced to nonzero number :** In DDC as and when any Standard subdivision reflects unusual importance in particular subject or subjects, such a SS concept is displaced to nonzero number. In other words such a concept takes shape of a subdivision of that particular subject and is used without a zero. In particular such a treatment is given to SS-09 used for historical, geographical treatment, e.g.:

362	Social welfare problems
.9	Historical, geographical, persons treatment.
372	Elementary education
.9	Historical, geographical, persons treatment.

3. **When the Meaning of SS is Specially Changed or Extended :** The Standard subdivisions may also be used with all such Standard subdivisions wherein DDC has specially changed or extended the meaning of Standard subdivisions. For example with subdivisions of:

370.1	Philosophy, theories, general aspect of Education,
669.02	Miscellany of extractive metallurgy.

Examples:

Title: Serial Publication on vocational education.

Base No		"
370.113	+	-05

C. No. 370.11305

Title: An index of hydrometallurgy

Base No		"
669.0283	+	-016

C. No. 669.0283016

PRACTICAL APPLICATION

The class numbers enumerated in the Schedules may be divided into two categories from the point of view of the use of Standard subdivisions:

i Class numbers under which instruction for the use of Standard subdivisions is provided.

ii Class numbers wherein no such instruction is available

1. CLASS NUMBERS UNDER WHICH INSTRUCTION TO USE SS IS PROVIDED

Under all such class numbers wherein there is need to use two or more zeros for SS, the instruction how to use SS is provided, e.g.

300 Social Sciences
Use 300.1-300.9 for standard subdivisions
375 Çurriculums
.0001-.0008 Standard subdivisions

It is, therefore, imperative for the classifier to verify before using the Standard subdivision if the instruction to use more zeros is provided under the class number or not.

THE INSTRUCTION TO USE - STANDARD SUBDIVISIONS - RATIONALE

The Standard subdivisions in DDC are enumerated in Table 1 with the help of a zero. In other words, it may be said that zero acts as a connecting symbol of SS which enables its free use with the class numbers enumerated in the Schedules. However, there are some exceptional situations when this zero is utilised by DDC to discharge the following different functions due to which it becomes necessary to provide specific instructions with regard to the use of Standard subdivisions.

1. A. WHEN ZERO IS USED FOR SUBDIVIDING DISCIPLINES/SUBJECTS

As a general rule DDC has used Indo-Arabic numerals 1-9 for subdividing the various disciplines and subjects in the Schedules, e.g.

340 Law
341 International law
.1 Sources of International law
.2 The World community
.3 Relations between states

However, there are subjects in the Schedules for which besides 1-9, 0 has also been utilised for enumerating their subdivisions, e.g.

342 Constitutional and administrative law
Use 342.001-342.009 for Standard subdivisions
.02 Basic instruments of governments

.023	Texts of constitutions
.024	Sources
.07	Election law

In this situation the instruction in regard to the use Standard subdivisions becomes necessary to avoid any possible conflict with Standard subdivisions enumerated using one zero in Table 1.

The instruction is obligatory for the classifier, otherwise two documents on two different subjects will have the same class numbers. The following example may help the classifier in understanding the need of this instruction:

Title: Study and teaching of Constitutional Law:

Class number if instruction is not followed	Correct class number when instruction is followed
342.07	342.007

1. B. WHEN ZERO IS USED FOR INDICATING AREAS

Examples

027	General libraries
.001-.009	Standard subdivisions
.01-.09	Geographical treatment Add to base number 027.0 notation 1-9 from Table 2

Title: Periodicals on general libraries

C. No. 027.005

Title: General libraries in Asia

C. No. 027.05

1. C. WHEN ZERO IS USED TO ADD TWO AREAS

Examples

382	International commerce (foreign trade)

.09 Historical, geographical treatment

Add to base number 382.09 notations 1-9 from Table 2... then for trade between two countries, regions, areas, places add † 0 and again add notation 1-9 from Table 2.

Title: Trade between United Kingdom and Asian countries

Base No.		Areas Table 2		Add		Areas Table 2
382.09	+	-41	+	0	+	-5

C. No. 382.094105

Title: Serial publications on international commerce of United Kingdom

Base No.		Areas Table 2		SS 1	SS as per instruction
382.09	+	-41	+	- 05	- 005

C. No. 382.0941005

(† footnote instruction directs to use 00 for SS)

1. D. WHEN ZERO IS USED FOR ADDING AREAS NOTATION AND HISTORICAL PERIODS FROM 930-990

Examples:

324 .9 Historical and geographical treatment of elections

.91-.99 Geographical treatment

Add to base number 324.9 notations 1-9 from Table 2...; then to the result add historical period numbers from appropriate sub-divisions of 930-990 ... In all cases use one 0* except 00* for North America and South America.

Title : Studies of voting behaviour in India after Independence

Base No.		Areas		Historical period of 930-990
324.9	+	-54	+	[954.]04

C. No. 324.95404

Title : Studies of voting behaviour in India - a survey

Base No.		Areas		SS	SS as per instruction
324.9	+	-54	+	-0723	-00723

C. No. 324.95400723

(* The footnote instruction directs to use 00 for SS)

1. E. WHEN ZERO IS USED FOR ADDING AREAS AND SUBJECT ENUMERATED IN THE SCHEDULES.

Examples:

338.9 Economic development and growth

.93-.99 Economic development and growth in specific continents, countries, localities.

Add to base number 338.9 notation 3-9 from Table 2..., then add 0* and to the result add the numbers following 338.92 in 338.922 - 338.927 ...

Title: Subsidies and grants in India

Base No.		Areas 2	Add		Add nos following 338.92
338.9	+	-54	+ 0	+	[338.92]2

C. No. 338.95402

Title: Economic planning and programmes in India - Chronological outlines

Base No.		Areas		SS		SS as per instruction
338.9	+	-54	+	-0202	+	- 00202

C. No. 338.95400202

(*footnote instruction directs to use 00 for SS)

1. F. WHEN ZERO IS USED FOR ADDING NOTATION OF TWO TABLES

Examples:

305.7 Language groups

Add to base number 305.7 notation 1-9 from Table 6. then add 0* and to the result add notation 1-9 from Table 2 ...

Title: Punjabi speaking people of South Asia

Base No.		Languages Table 6		Add		Areas Table 2
305.7	+	-9142	+	0*	+	-54

C. No. 305.79142054

Title: Descriptive research on Punjabi speaking people.

Base No.		Table 6		SS	SS as per instruction
305.7	+	-9142	+	0723	-00723

C. No. 305.7914200723

(* footnote instruction directs to use 00 for SS)

METHODS USED FOR PROVIDING THE INSTRUCTION TO USE SS

(i) **Through the specific instruction under the class number itself, e.g.:**

345 Criminal Law

Use 345.001-345.009 for Standard subdivisions

(ii) **Through enumeration, e.g.:**

320	Political Science (politics and government)
.01	Philosophy and theory
.02-.08	Standard subdivisions

This also indicates that two zeros are to be used for SS.

(iii) **Through Special Tables, e.g.:**

616.1-616.9	Specific diseases Except for additions, changes...add to the notation for the each term identified by * as follows:-
001	Philosophy and theory
003-006	Standard subdivisions

(iv) **Through * (Asterisk) or † (dagger):** which directs the classifier to read the footnote instruction "Use extra 0 s for standard subdivisions; see instruction at the beginning of Table 1"

This method is used generally when one 0 is used for the followings:

1. for adding notation of Table 2
2. for adding two areas
3. for adding areas and subjects enumerated in the Schedules
4. for adding notation of two Table.

All these are already explained with examples under the heading "Instruction to Use SS - Rationale'

2. CLASS NUMBERS WHERE INSTRUCTION IS NOT PROVIDED

If no instruction or enumeration in regard to the use of Standard subdivision is available under a class number, then the classifier is free to add directly the Standard subdivisions to that particular class number, e.g.

Title: Serial publications on Hindu religion

294.5 Hindu religion + -05 Serial publications (Table 1)

C. No. 294.505

However, where no instruction to use two or more zeros is provided, the classifier may have to omit zero or zeros from the class number of a subject before adding to it the Standard subdivisions notation. Because DDC uses zero or zeros at the end of a class number if it is less than three digited, e.g.:

100	Philosophy
200	Religion
310	Statistics
330	Economics

It means the significant digits denoting the subjects are 1 Philosophy, 2 Religion, 31 Statistics and 33 Economics and the zero or zeros are added after these significant digits only to make them three digited numbers. Otherwise, these zeros have no semantic value. So if a Standard subdivision notation is to be added to a class number ending with zero or zeros, these are to be omitted before adding to it the Standard subdivisions notation, e.g.*

Title: General books of unusual and curious facts.

Base No.		**SS Table 1**
03[0]	+	-02

C. No. 030.2

Title: Research on life sciences in India

Base No.		**SS base No. Table 1**		**Areas Table 2**
5[0]	+	-0720	+	-54

C. No. 570.72054

DO NOT USE STANDARD SUBDIVISIONS

Due to its enumerative nature DDC has taken help of various types of notes to adjust subjects which the Editorial Board think lack literary warrant or unable to decide what their ultimate class should be. Such subjects are clubbed under a class number and are kept in waiting list till in future revised edition they may be provided a class of their own on the basis of expansion device e.g. in Edition 20

302.13	Social choice including attraction, influence
.14	Social participation Example: Cooperation, voluntarism

In the Editor's Introduction the classifier has been specifically directed that Standard subdivisions can not be added for topics in standing room nor are other number building technique allowed'.

EDITIONS 19 AND 20: WHERE THE EDITIONS DIFFER

1. In Edition 20 the Table of Precedence has been extended by adding some Standard subdivisions like -0221, 0218, -08, -0112, -075 and -09.

* Square brackets are used in all examples to indicate the numbers following or numbers which are not to be added.

2. As per general practice of DDC Editorial Policy Committee in Edition 20 numbers for many Standard subdivisions have also been discontinued and many new ones have been added. Few such Standard subdivisions which need specific mention are:

-03 Dictionaries, encyclopaedias, concordances. The provisions to add languages notation from Table 6 of Edition 19 has been discontinued in the new edition.

-07 The nomenclature has been changed in Edition 20 from 'Study and teaching' to 'Education, research, related topics' However, enumeration of subdivisions remain the same.

-08 History and description of the subject among groups of persons of Edition 19 had only two subdivisions -088 and -089. In Edition 20 the notation -08 now reads as History and description with respect to kinds of persons and has many more subdivisions from -081 to -089. Moreover, these subdivisions are similar to the subdivisions of Table 7 'Persons' from -04 to -08, but in Table 1 these have been much more extended.

-09 Historical, geographical treatment of Edition 19 has the following *additions* in Edition 20:

(i) -09 now reads as Historical, geographical, persons treatment.

(ii) Special Tables have been provided under -0901-0905 Historical periods and 093-099 treatment by specific continents ... These Tables have such following subdivisions:

01 Forecasting and forecasts
02 Statistics and illustrations
05 Periodicals
07 Museums, collections...

CONCLUSION

The following guidelines may be kept in view before using Standard subdivisions (SS):

(i) When instruction is not given - verify before using SS if the class number ends with zero or zeros, omit them before adding the SS to that class number.

(ii) If instruction is given - read carefully the instruction which may be under the class number or in the footnote indicated through * (asterisk) or † (dagger) and then add zeros to SS before adding it to the class number.

(iii) It should be kept in view that in synthesised class number the SS is applicable to entire class number and not to any of its element or part;

(iv) Do not use SS to a subject for which broad class number is to be used, and co-extensive class number for that subject is not available in the Schedules or may not be devised using various other number building methods;

(v) Use the extended and modified Standard subdivisions in place of subdivisions of Table 1, with specific subjects -026-0269 under 342-347 Law of specific jurisdiction and -0202-079 under 796.332 American football.

(vi) Preference should be given to an enumerated standard subdivision; and

(vii) Never add a standard subdivision to a subject which is clubbed and kept in a waiting list under a specific class number.

Practical Problems

1. Diplomatic languages.
2. Classification of Invertebrates.
3. Study and Teaching of Constitutional Law.
4. Journal of Philosophy.
5. Historians of India.
6. Teaching of DDC through television classes.
7. International organisations in photo journalism.
8. Teaching of Ramayana in Indian schools.
9. Concordance of Bhagwat Gita.
10. Apptitude test for military personnel.
11. An Index of non-religious subjects treated in Bible.

12. Scientific principles used in the preparation of bibliographies.
13. Descriptive research on Indian foreign relations.
14. Indian election law guide.
15. History of sports and games among Koreans.

Solutions

1. 401.3
2. 592.0012
3. 342.007
4. 105
5. 954.00702
6. 025.43107153
7. 070.490601
8. 294.5922071254
9. 294.592403
10. 153.9400088355
11. 220.800016
12. 011.0015
13. 327.5400723
14. 342.540702648
15. 796.089957

IV

TABLE 2
GEOGRAPHIC AREAS, HISTORICAL PERIODS, PERSONS

The notations for geographical divisions, historical periods and persons are enumerated in Table 2. The main criteria used by DDC for the formation of geographical divisions are:

(1) Zonal regions, e.g. Frigid Zones, Torrid Zones, etc.

(2) Physiographic regions, e.g. Plane regions, coastal regions, etc.

(3) Types of vegetation, e.g. Forests, deserts, etc.

(4) Air and water, e.g. Atmosphere, oceans and seas, etc.

(5) Socio-economic regions, e.g. Western block, urban regions, rural regions etc.

(6) Other kinds of terrestrial regions, e.g. Eastern hemisphere, Western hemisphere, oceans and sea basins.

(7) Space.

(8) Continents, countries, localities and extraterrestrial worlds.

The notations -01-09 of Table 2 are allotted in the following manner:

-01-05	Historical periods (Edition 20)
-1	Areas, regions, places in general
-2	Persons
-3	The ancient world
-4	Europe Western Europe
-5	Asia Orient Far East
-6	Africa
-7	North America
-8	South America

-9 Other parts of world and extraterrestrial worlds, Pacific Ocean islands.

The notations -01-05 historical periods are to be subdivided on the basis of notation - 0901-0905 of Table 1.

In general, classifier has to take help of the Relative Index to know the notation for the required geographical isolate. However, the single level summaries given at the beginning of each continent, country, and state provide an overview of the subdivisions, which may also help in locating the required areas notations.

In Edition 20, besides various modifications, extensions, there are two major additions:-

(i) 01-05 Historical Periods, and

(ii) the multilevel summaries for -4 Europe and -7 North America, which provide a clear picture of the areas divisions enumerated under -4 and -7 using numbers -1-9.

PRACTICAL APPLICATION

Areas notation do not constitute by themselves a class number. These are to be added to the class numbers enumerated in the Schedules or when so directed with numbers from other Tables.

METHODS TO ADD AREAS NOTATION

The following two methods are used to add areas notations to class numbers enumerated in the Schedules:-

1. Through instruction
2. Through -09 Standard subdivision (Table 1)

1. TO ADD AREAS NOTATION THROUGH INSTRUCTION

The notation of Table 2 may be used directly with any number from the Schedules through the instruction given under that number for adding Areas notation from Table 2. The classifier, however, may be directed to add Areas notation from:

-01-9 (Ed. 20 only) or

-1-9 or -3-9 or -4-9

Note: In Edition 20 there are two minor modifications/extensions with regard to the terms and instruction used to indicate the Areas notation.

1.1 Addition of the term Persons:

In Edition 20 the subdivisions Historical, geographical treatment has been extended to Historical, geographical, persons treatment.

1.2 Modification in the language of the instruction:

Ed. 19 Add Areas notation...from Table 2 to base number.

Ed. 20 Add to base number...notation...from Table 2.

To Note: It may, therefore, be *noted* that the language as is used in Edition 20 would be used in this book.

PRACTICE-STEPS TO BE USED

(1) write the class number of the document to be classified;

(2) see the instruction provided for Areas notation;

(3) see what is the base number to which Areas notation is to be added;

(4) correct the class number according to the base number so provided;

(5) bring Areas notation needed from Table 2;

(6) add it to the base number.

Examples:

Title: General libraries in India

027 General libraries

027.01-.09 Geographical treatment

Add to base number 027.0 notation 1-9 from Table 2

-54 India (Table 2)

Base No.		**Table 2**
027.0	+	-54

C. No. 027.054

Title: Public libraries in Rajasthan

027.4 Public libraries

027.43-.49 Treatment by specific continents, countries, localities

Add to base number 027.4 notation 3-9 from Table 2

-544 Rajasthan (Table 2)

Base No.		Table 2
027.4	+	-544

C. No. 027.4544

Points to Note:

1. The classifier should keep in mind that in the Add Areas... instruction he is required to follow two specific directions- (i) regarding the Base number, which makes imperative for the classifier to add areas notation only after the base number as is given in the instruction; (ii) regarding the areas notation which may be added from -1-9 or from 3-9 or from 4-9. If he does not follow these directions the devised class number may be wrong.
2. It is also necessary for the classifier to know that the instruction for 'Add Areas notation' may be given in the beginning under the required class number, e.g.:

027.1 Private and family libraries

Add to base number 027.1 notation 1-9 from Table 2

or

Under any one of its subdivisions, e.g.

342 Constitutional and administrative law

342.02-.09 (Subdivisions enumerated)

3-.9 Specific jurisdictions and areas

Add to base number notation 3-9 from Table 2.

Thus, while classifying a document the classifier should verify all the subdivisions of that particular class number which is required for classifying the document to find out whether any one of its subdivisions has been used for providing the geographical treatment to that class number. It is necessary to check all the subdivisions of that class number to find out under which subdivision the instruction for the use of areas is provided for that subject. The classifier should not think that the instruction will necessarily be given immediately under the class number itself.

3. The classifier should note the basic difference between the instructions provided for Standard subdivisions and for the Areas. The instruction for Standard subdivisions will always necessarily be provided under the class number to which it is to be added. In case of Areas the instruction may be given immediately under the class number itself or the instruction may be provided under any subdivisions of that class number which may be particularly used for bringing Areas notation only.

2. TO ADD AREAS NOTATION THROUGH -09 HISTORICAL, GEOGRAPHICAL TREATMENT (TABLE 1. STANDARD SUBDIVISIONS)

With all those class numbers of the Schedules, where instruction to add Areas notation from Table 2 is not given, help of -09 of Standard subdivisions is taken. In other words Areas notation of Table 2 may be added to any class number enumerated in the Schedules through the notation -09 of Standard subdivision even if no instruction to add Areas notation is provided. The instructions to add Areas notations from Table 2 are provided under the following subdivisions of -09:

-091 Treatment by areas, regions, places in general
Add to base number -091 the numbers following -1 in -11-19 from Table 2

-092 Persons

-0922 Collected treatment
Add to base number -0922 notation -3-9 from Table 2

-093-099 Treatment by specific continents, countries...
Add to base number -09 notation 3-9 from Table 2.

This means that with the base number -09 notations -1-9 from Table 2 may be added to all those numbers of the Schedules, wherein no instruction to add areas notation from Table 2 is provided.

Caution : Basically -09 is a notation from Standard subdivisions Table 1. Therefore, the classifier while using Areas notation through -09 should follow all the rules applicable to Standard subdivisions. As and when the classifier is adding Areas notation through -09 he has to verify whether instruction to use two or more zeros with Standard subdivisions is given or if he has to omit the zero or zeros before adding Standard subdivisions to that class number if the class number ends with zero or zeros.

PRACTICE-STEPS TO BE USED

(1) write the class number of the document to be classified;

(2) verify if instruction to 'Add Areas notation' is given;

If not

(3) then classifier has to take help of -09 Standard subdivision (Table 1);

(4) verify if instruction to use two or more zeros with Standard subdivisions is given:

If Yes

(4.1) then classifier will have to use the number of zeros with -09 accordingly;

(4.2) write down -09 and add to it number of zeros as per instruction;

(4.3) then add to it "Areas" notation 1-9 from Table 2.

When no instruction is provided for use of Standard Subdivisions:

(5) write down -09 and add to it the required notation from Table 2;

(6) thus the areas notation is ready to be added to the class number. But before adding this notation to the class number omit zero or zeros if the class number ends with zero or zeros.

Examples:

Title: Women workers in India

331.4 Women workers
(Instruction to add "Areas" notation not given)

-54 India (Table 2).

As instruction to add "Areas" notation is not given -54 can not be added to 331.4 directly but it can be added through -09 of Standard subdivisions, e.g.:

331.4 Women workers

-093-099 Treatment by specific continents, countries, localities; extraterrestrial worlds (Table 1).
Add to base number -09 notation 3-9 from Table 2

-54 India (Table 2)

Base No.		SS (Table 1)		Areas (Table 2)
331.4	+	-09	+	-54

C. No. 331.40954

Title: Christian religious congregations in India.

250 Local Christian church and Christian religious orders.

255 Religious congregations and orders
Use 255.001-255.009 for Standard subdivisions

-54 India (Table 2)

Base No.		SS	SS as per Inst.		Areas (Table 2)
255	+	-09	-009	+	-54

C. No. 255.00954

USE OF TWO AREAS NOTATION TOGETHER

In case a document deals with two or more continents, countries or localities, etc. the classifier is required to choose one of the Areas notation on the basis of its importance or need of the library. However DDC has provided specific instruction in Areas Table as well as under certain class numbers in the Schedules, which to some extent makes possible the use of Two Areas together.

TWO AREAS EXPLAINED

The term Two Areas means using two Areas notation together which are enumerated;

(a) under - 1

(b) under - 3-9

or

(c) both areas notation enumerated under - 3-9

In other words using together :

Areas notation enumerated under -1 + Areas notation enumerated under 3-9 Or Areas notation enumerated under 3-9 + Areas notation enumerated under 3-9.

USE OF AREAS NOTATION ENUMERATED UNDER - 1 PLUS AREAS NOTATION ENUMERATED UNDER 3-9 TOGETHER

If the classifier has to use the Areas notation enumerated under - 1 and Areas notation from 3-9 together, he has to take help of the two instructions given by DDC in Areas Table for this purpose.

TWO INSTRUCTIONS

First Instruction

First Instruction is similar in both the editions 19 and 20. The instruction is given under - 1 which denotes Areas, regions, places in general. This instructions is as follows:

If desired, add to each number as follows:

-03-09 Treatment by continent, country, locality

Add 0 to base number and then add notation -3-9 from this table

Analysis: Here the base number means the Areas notation enumerated under - 1 e.g.:

-152	Forests
-154	Deserts
-1734	Rural regions

after this base number add 0, e.g.:
-1520
-1540
-17340

and then add to this the required Areas notation from -3-9, e.g.:

-54 India	-	152054
	-	154054
	-	1734054

This areas notation is to be added to the required class number enumerated in the Schedules e.g.:

364 Criminology

Crime and its alleviation

.9 Historical geographical, persons treatment of crime and its alleviation.

Add to base number 364.9 notation 01-9 from Table 2

Table 2

- 1 Areas, regions, places in general

-03-09 Treatment by continent, country, locality

Add 0 to base number and then add notation 3-9 from this table

-1734 Rural regions

-add 0 to 1734

-17340

then add 3-9 i.e. 54

Title: A study of crimes in rural regions of India

Base No.		**Add Areas notation - 1**		**Add zero**		**Add Areas notation 3-9**
364.9	+	-1734	+	0	+	-54

C. No. 364.91734054

361 Social problems and social welfare in general

.9 Historical, geographical, persons treatment

Add to base number 361.9 notation from Table 2

Table 2 -1812 Western

Add 0 to -1812

-18120

then add 3-9 i.e. -5475 - Gujarat

Title: A study of social problems of Western Gujarat

Base No.		Add Areas - 1		Add zero		Add Areas 3-9
361.9	+	-1812	+	0	+	-5475

C. No. 361.9181205475

Second instruction: The second instruction differs in Editions 19 and 20.

Edition 19

In Edition 19 the second instruction is available under -3-9 and also under different continents, e.g.:

Under -3-9, Specific continents, countries, localities; extraterrestrial words

If desired add to each number as follows:

009 Regional treatment

Add to 009 the number following - 1 in - 11 - 19

(An alternative treatment is shown under - 1)

Analysis: Here the base number will be the Areas notation enumerated under 3-9, e.g.:

-5 Asia

-54 India

after this base number add 009, e.g.:

-5009

-54009

and then add to this numbers following - 1. It means the classifier has to omit the digit 1 before adding its subdivisions to the above number, e.g.:

[*1] 52	Forests	-5400952
[-1] 54	Deserts	-5400954
[-1] 734	Rural regions	-54009734

This Areas notation now may be added to the required class number enumerated in the Schedules.

Under different continents, e.g.:

-4 Europe Western Europe

-4009 Regional treatment

Add to base number -4009 the numbers following -1 in -11 - 18 of this Table

Base No.		numbers following - 1
-4009	+	[-1] 713 Western block
-4009713		

This Areas notation now may be added to the required class number

Analysis of the Two Instructions

(1) both the instructions allow to add two Areas notation together i.e. to add Areas notation:
   (a) one Areas notation from -1
   (b) and another Area notation from 3-9
(2) following is the difference in the use of these two instructions i.e.
   (a) instruction given under - 1 uses zero as the connecting symbol i.e. after the Area notation used from - 1 zero is to be added. Then after this the required Areas notation enumerated under -3-9 is to be added.
   (b) the instruction under -3-9 and under Areas notation for different continents directs the classifier to use

* Square brackets are used in all examples to indicate numbers following or numbers which are not to be added.

connecting symbol 009 to connect areas notation following - 1.

It means in Edition 19, there are two alternatives for devising the same Areas notation e.g.:

Title: Crimes in the cities of India

364 Criminology
364.9 Historical, geographical treatment..
Add to base number 364.9 notation 1-9 from Table 2

First Method (Applicable in both Editions 19 and 20)

Base No.		Add Areas notation - 1		Add zero		Add areas notation 3-9
364.9	+	-1732	+	0	+	-54

C. No. 364.91732054

Second Method (Applicable only in Edition 19)

Base no.		Add Areas notation 3-9		Add 009		Add Areas notation following - 1
364.9	+	-54	+	009	+	[-1] 732

C. No. 364.954009732

However, in libraries which are using Edition 19, the option rests with the classifier to choose one of the alternatives according to the needs of the library or of documents.

Edition 20

In Edition 20 *No* instruction is given under -3-9. However, in the Manual it has been clearly stated under T2 - 1 that 'within a single country or place these general regions are classed in the general number for the country or place'. Except in the disciplines geography and history, with which the appropriate subdivisions of - 1 may be added as per provision under 0091-0098 of special

Table for 930-990. 'In all other disciplines this is done only as an option that is not followed by the Decimal Classification Division.

INSTRUCTION UNDER CONTINENTS

In both the editions 19 and 20, the instruction to add Areas notation following - 1 is available under different continents also. However, the base number after which the Areas notation following -1 is to be added is different in both the editions.

	Edition 19		*Edition 20*
-4	Europe	-4	Europe
-4009	Regional treatment Add to base number -4009 the numbers following - 1 in - 11 - 18 of this table	-4091	Regional treatment (formerly 4009) Add to base number -4091 the numbers following - 1 in - 11 -18 of this table

Libraries changing from Edition 19 to 20 would have to make necessary corrections in the base number.

USE OF TWO AREAS NOTATION ENUMERATED UNDER - 3-9

As a general rule DDC does not permit the use of two continents or countries or localities together. However, in all such subjects or disciplines where the need for two Areas is apparent the necessary instruction in this regard is given in the instruction itself. DDC also provides the citation order in the following manner:-

> 'give priority in notation to the nation emphasised. If emphasis is equal, give priority to the one coming first in the sequence of areas notation'.

(Option: Give priority in notation to the nation requiring local emphasis).

Examples:

Title: Foreign relations between India and United States

327	International relations
.3-9	Foreign relations of specific nation

Add to base number 327 notation 3-9 from Table 2, e.g.:

327 + -54 India (Table 2) = 327.54

then for the relations between that nation and another nation or region add 0, e.g.: 327.540

and to the result add notation 1-9 from Table 2, e.g.:

C. No. 327.54073

Here the notation -54 India is given priority to give local emphasis.

Title: Economic cooperation between Japan and France.

337 International Economics

.3-.9 Foreign economic policies and relations of specific jurisdictions and groups of jurisdictions.

Add to base number 337 notation 3-9 from Table 2; then for economic relations between two jurisdictions or groups of jurisdictions add 0 and to the result add notation 1-9 from Table 2

Base No.		**Add notation 3-9**		**Add 0**		**Add notation 1-9**
337	+	-44	+	0	+	-52

C. No. 337.44052

Here the emphasis is equal, priority to -44 France is given, as it comes first in the sequence of Areas notation.

However, when the sequence of the two areas is self explanatory, then the separate specific instruction for order of precedence is not given. e.g.:

Title: Emigration from India to European countries

325.2 Emigration

.23-.29 Emigration from specific continents, countries, localities

Ed. 19 Add "Areas" notation 3-9 from Table 2 to base number 325.2 e.g. emigration from Japan 325.252; then add 09 and to the result add "Areas" notation 1-9 from Table 2 for place entered e.g., emigration from Japan to United States 325.2520973

Ed. 20 Add to base number 325.2 notation 3-9 from Table 2, e.g. emigration from Japan 325.252. Then add 09 and to the result add notation 3-9 from Table 2 for place entered e.g. emigration from Japan to United States 325.2520973

Base No.		Areas Table 2 (from)		Add		Areas Table 2 (to)
325.2	+	-54	+	09	+	-4

C. No. 325.254094

USE OF THE NOTATION OF TABLE 2 THROUGH OTHER TABLES

Areas notation of Table 2 has used particularly by all the Tables for providing geographic elements to their concepts. A few such examples are as follows;

Table 1 Standard Subdivisions

Besides -09 which is being used as a connecting symbol for adding Areas notation, there are other Standard sub-divisions also which are subdivided on the basis of Areas notation of Table 2 e.g.:

-023 The subject as a profession

Add to base number -023 notation 1 or 3-9 from Table 2.

Title: Library and Information Science as a profession in under developed countries

Base No.		SS Table 1		Areas Table
02[0]	+	-023	+	-1724

C. No. 020.231724

Table 3-A/3-C Additional for literature

-32 places
Add to -32 notation 1-9 from Table 2. e.g.
Rajasthan -32544

Title: Collections of Hindi literature describing the culture and civilization of Rajasthan.

Base No.		Table 3 Base No.		Table 3-A/3-C		Areas Table 2
891.43	+	-080	+	-32	+	-544

C. No. 891.4308032544

Table 5. Racial, Ethnic, National Groups

-9275-9276 National groups of Arabs
Add to base number -927 notation 5-6 from Table 2, e.g.:

Title: Psychology of Iraqis:

Base No.		Table 5		Areas Table 2
155.84	+	-927	+	-567

C. No. 155.84927567

CAUTION

(1) While adding Areas notation with the help of the notation - 09 of S.S.; verify the class number of the subject in the Schedules as some *note* or *instruction* in this regard may be given under it. For example:-

027.7 College and University libraries

027.7 Historitical and geo.....treatment
class specific institutions in 027.73 - 027.79 (not in 027. 7093 - 027.7099)

340 Law

340.09 Historical and geographical treatment

.[093]	Treatment by specific...in ancient world Do not use class in 340.53
591	Zoology
591.09	Historical and geographical treatment of Zoology Class geographical treatment in 591.9

(2) The specific subject may have been enumerated on the basis of geographical characteristics and the base number of it may include the number of continent or country. For example:-

061-068	General Organisations
061.1	In Canada
062	In England Add to base number 062 numbers following -42 in -421 - 428 from Table 2.
	or
310	General Statistics
314	Of Asia*
315	Of Asia*

The symbol* directs to add as instructed under 314 - 319, where in the instruction - Add Areas notation to base number 31 the notation -3-9 from Table 2 is given.

(3) That Areas notations may be extended further on the basis of the subdivisions of that specific subdivisions e.g.

342 - 348	Law of Specific Branches*
342. 3-.9	Law of Specific jurisdiction
342	Constitutional Law + - 54 India + 024 sources
342.54024	Sources of Indian constitutional Law
	Or
	On the basis of Special Table, e.g.
328.4 - .9	Legislative process in specific jurisdiction Add to base number 328 notation -4-9 from Table 2
	then add as follows:-

* *See also* Chapter XI pages 133-135

01 Journals
02 Debates
03 Abstracts

Title : Debates of Legislative process in India
C. No. **328.5402**

Or

by *Chronological Divisions*

Title : History of Mughal India
C. No. **954.025**

(4) Geographical and Historical treatment may be shown as a subdivision. e.g.:

324.9	Historical and geographical treatment of elections
591.9	Geographical treatment of animals (Fauna)

(5) Two different numbers may be used for historical and geographical treatment e.g.:

592.009	Historical and geographical treatment of the study of invertebrates
592.09	Geographical treatment of invertebrates Zoology

It is therefore, necessary to read the instructions and verify the enumeration of the class number for the specific subject before adding to it the areas notation

Practical Problems

1. Restaurants of Goa
2. Diseases among children in under developed countries
3. Ranches and farms of animals in Brazil
4. Vocational interest tests in India
5. Participation of Great Britain in World War I.
6. The beginning of open economy system in India.

7. Technological unemployment in developing countries.
8. Credit and loan functions of insurance companies in India.
9. Ramkrishna movement in Europe.
10. American foreign investments in Germany.
11. Welfare work in Gujarat.
12. Immigrant workers from Bhutan in West Bengal.
13. Economic assistance by India to Ethiopia.
14. Art galleries, museums and private collections in India.
15. Collections by Sudhir Dhar: An Indian cartoonist.

Solutions

1. 647.9554799
2. 618.9200091724
3. 638.010981
4. 153.94000954
5. 940.5341
6. 330.1220954
7. 331.137042091723
8. 332.380954
9. 294.555094
10. 332.67373043
11. 361.95475
12. 331.62549805414
13. 338.9154063
14. 708.954
15. 741.5954

V

TABLE 3
SUBDIVISIONS OF INDIVIDUAL LITERATURES

Table 3 and its supplementaries are specifically designed to meet the various requirements of literatures of specific languages enumerated in the main class 800 Literature from 810-890. The notations of this Table do not constitute class numbers by themselves but are to be:-

1. added to the individual literatures identified by *(asterisk) enumerated from 810-890 in the Schedules;
2. added to the class numbers from 808 to 809, (only where necessary instruction in this regard is given).

Editions 19 and 20

In Edition 20 Table 3 has been bifurcated into *Three* Tables: Table 3-A, Table 3-B and Table 3-C, whereas in Edition 19 Table 3 has only one supplementary 3-A. However, there is no difference in Editions 19 and 20 in so far as the enumeration of concepts, use of notations, necessary instructions and the number devised on the basis of these tables is concerned. Following comparison makes it more clear:

	Ed. 19	Ed. 20
1. Rules and steps to use Table 3 and its supplementaries	Table 3	Table 3
2. Subdivisions for works by or about individual authors	Table 3	Table 3-A
3. Subdivisions for works by or about more than one author	Table 3	Table 3-B
4. Notations for additional elements	Table 3-A	Table 3-C

In Edition 20 allotting one table to *individual author* and another to works by or about *more than one author* has made the task of the classifier much easier. In Edition 19 it was a little bit confusing as these were to be classed as per directions given under different numbers in this regard.

INDIVIDUAL WORKS

WORKS BY OR ABOUT INDIVIDUAL AUTHORS - BROAD GUIDELINES

I. Literary work of an individual author is to be classed by language in which work is originally written, regardless of country;

II. that such a work is to be classified with the form in which the individual author writes the literature;

III. if the works by an individual author cover two or more forms of literature, class the work with the form with which the author is mainly identified;

IV. that after form number, period number may be added;

V. that if the works of a individual author is neither limited to, nor identified by one specific form, then the works of the individual author may be classed in -8 Miscellaneous writings;

VI. that the notations enumerated for specific features, specific kinds or types of specific forms of literature are not applicable to works of individual authors;

VII. that the base number always means the number for specific literature in which the individual author writes his literary works and as provided in Schedules from 810-890;

VIII. that the main elements required for classifying literary works of an individual author are.

Language Number:	Provided in the Schedules from 810-890
Form Number:	1-8 from Table 3 (Edition 19) Table 3-A (Edition 20)
Period Number:	From Period Table as under specific literature in 810-890;

IX. that from the point of view of practical classification the works of individual authors may be divided in to:

IX (a) Works in one specific form

IX (b) Works regardless of form.

WORKS BY OR ABOUT AN INDIVIDUAL AUTHOR IN ONE SPECIFIC FORM

PRACTICE-STEPS TO BE USED

Language Number

Step 1. Write down the base number for the language of specific literature from the Schedules in 810-890. The number should be identified by *(asterisk) e.g.

810 * American literature in English

Base number: 81

Or

as enumerated in Schedules

891.2 * Sanskrit

Form Number

Step 2. Add to this number the form number in which the literature is written from Table 3 (Ed. 19), Table 3-A (Ed. 20) e.g.:

Base No.	**+ -1-8 Specific Forms**		
81	+ - 1 Poetry	=	811 American English poetry
891.2	+ - 2 Drama	=	891.22 Sanskrit drama

Period Number

Step 3. If the specific subject deals with literature of a specific period, then the classifier has to verify under the specific literature if period table is available or not. If *Yes,* add the period number after the form number, if *No.* treat the number as complete, e.g.:

Title: Child Harold's Pilgrimage by Lord Byron (English poet of Ramantic era)

820 *English and Old English (Anglo-Saxon) literature

Base number for English 82

PERIOD TABLE FOR ENGLISH

7 1800-1837

Class here Romantic era

Poetry -1 (Table 3/3-A)

Base No.		**Poetry**		**Period**
82	+	-1	+	7

C. No. 821.7

Title: Early 20th century Punjabi fiction

	891.42	*Punjabi
Ed. 19 Table 3 / Ed. 20 Table 3-A	-3	Fiction
	-31-39	Specific periods Add to -3 the notations from the period table for the specific literature in 810-890
Schedules	891.42	Punjabi Use period table under 891.4
	891.4	Modern Indic literature... Period Table for specific...
	5	1895-1950

Base No.		**Fiction**		**Period No.**
891.42	+	-3	+	5

C. No. 891.4235

IF THERE IS NO APPLICABLE PERIOD TABLE

Title: 14th century Sanskrit drama

891.2 *Sanskrit

(Not applicable Period Table)

Ed. 19 Table 3 / **Ed. 20** Table 3-A	-2	Drama Add to -2 the notation from the period table for specific literature in 810-890, e.g...; If there is *no applicable period table* add nothing to -2.

Base No.		**Drama**
891.2	+	-2

C. No. 891.22

Analysis

The classifier may add period number to specific literature only when period table is provided in the Schedules under 810-890 for that specific literature. If *No* period table is applicable, then classifier is required to treat the number as complete and add nothing to form number.

William Shakespeare

Under 822.33 ready made class numbers are available for works by or about Shakespeare. The classifier has the option to use either the above described provisions or the ready made numbers for classifying works by and about Shakespeare. The ready made class numbers are, e.g.:

Title : Biography of Shakespeare

C. No. 822.33B

Title: Critical appraisal of Hamlet

C. No. 822.33T8

Two digited numbers are used for books written by Shakespeare. e.g.:

822.33 P3	Merchant of Venice
822.33 P4	Critical evaluation of Merchant of Venice.

-8 MISCELLANEOUS WRITINGS

WORKS BY OR ABOUT INDIVIDUAL AUTHORS REGARDLESS OF FORM

One of the directions provided under -1-8 specific forms relates to such individual authors who are writing in many forms and, therefore, may not be identified specifically with one specific form. This direction is in the form of option which states "Class description, critical appraisal, biography, single and collected works of all individual authors regardless of form in -8".

Similar option is also available under -8 miscellaneous writings which states 'Class here description, critical appraisal, biography, single and collected works of all individual authors regardless of form, prefer -1-8'.

If the classifier opts to class works of an individual author regardless of form under -8 Miscellaneous writings, then the *Procedure* used for number building would be as follows:

Title: Reminiscences of a Greek author of early 20th century

889*		Modern Greek	*Schedules*
		Period Table	
32		1900-1945	
Ed. 19	Table 3	-8	Miscellaneous writings
Ed. 20	Table 3-A	81-89	Specific periods
			Add to -8 the notation from period table for the specific literature in 810-890... then add further as follows: 03 Diaries, journals, reminiscences

Base No.		**Form**		**Specific period**		**Reminiscences as under -81-89**
889	+	-8	+	32	+	03

C. No. 889.83203

PRACTICE - STEPS TO BE USED

1. Write the base number of the specific literature from the Schedules, e.g. 889.
2. Add to this from Table 3 (Ed. 19), 3-A (Ed. 20) notation -8, e.g. 889.8
3. Add to this period number from the Schedules (under the notation -8 (Ed. 19) -81-89 (Ed. 20) instruction to add specific period ... is given) e.g. 889.832.

4. This instruction also directs to use subdivisions of -8 e.g. 889.83203.

WHEN THERE IS NO APPLICABLE PERIOD TABLE

Different provisions are prescribed in Editions 19 and 20 for works on such specific literatures for which no period table is available in the Schedules in 810-890.

Edition 19: Table 3

-81-89 Miscellaneous writings of specific periods

The last paragraph under this number directs the classifier that:

'*If there is no period table,* class quotations epigrams, anecdotes of all periods in -802; diaries, journals, reminiscences of all periods in -803; experimental and non-formalised works of all periods in -807; prose literature of all periods in -808'.

Edition 20: Table 3-A

-81-89 specific periods

'If there is no applicable period, add nothing to -8'

The above direction indicates that the provisions of the Edition 19 have been discontinued in Edition 20 and classifier is not permitted to add subdivisions of -81-89 to specific literature without specific period.

Examples:

Title: 18th century prose literature in Sanskrit

891.2 + -808 = 891.2808 (Ed. 19)

891.2 + -8 = 891.28 (Ed. 20)

Option: The Option under -81-89 in Edition 20 permits to use period numbers from periods tables for specific countries in the following manner

Title: Anecdotes in English by an Indian author of 18th century

828	+	02	=	828.02 **(Ed. 19)**
828	×	×	=	828 **(Ed. 20)**
In 828 +		-102	=	In 828.102 when option used

MORE THAN ONE AUTHOR (COLLECTED WORKS)

WORKS BY OR ABOUT MORE THAN ONE AUTHOR-BROAD GUIDELINES

I. that this category covers collected works of more than one author writing in one specific language;

II. that such a work is to be classed with specific form in which the collected work is written;

III. that if such a work is neither limited nor identified by one specific form then it may be classed in -8 Miscellaneous writings;

IV. that such a work may be subdivided on the basis of specific periods, scopes, kinds or types of specific forms of literature;

V. that to classify such a work, subdivisions of two different tables are to be used:

Ed. 19 Table 3 + Table 3-A

Ed. 20 Table 3-B + Table 3-C

VI. that the classifier may Note that in so far as the enumeration of subdivisions, notations and the procedure for their use is concerned, there is *no difference in Editions 19 and 20;*

VII. that from the point of view of practical classification the works by or about more than one author may be divided in to:

VII(a) Collected works *not* restricted to one specific form

VII(b) Collected works restricted to one form

COLLECTED WORKS NOT RESTRICTED TO ONE FORM

For a literary work by or about more than one author not restricted to one specific form, the subdivisions required are:

-08 Collections

-09 History, description, critical appraisal

-08 COLLECTIONS - PROCEDURE TO BE USED

-08 Collections

Ed. 19	Add to -080 the notation -01-99 from Table 3-A
Ed. 20	Add 0 to -08; then to the result add notation -001 -99 from Table 3-C

So in both the editions the base number is -080, if notation from Table 3-A (Ed. 19), 3-C (Ed. 20) are to be added after -08 collections.

PRACTICE-STEPS TO BE USED

1. write the base number for specific literature as provided in 810-890 identified by*;
2. add to the above base number -080 from Table 3 (Ed. 19), 3-B (Ed. 20);
3. then add required notation from Table 3-A/3-C;
4. if the required notation from Table 3-A/3-C is from -01-09 specific period, then add only 0 after 080 from Table 3-A/ 3-C; i.e. 0800; then
5. after this add number from period table given for specific literature in the Schedules under 810-890;

Examples:

Title: An anthology of Bengali literature.

Base No.		**Collections Table 3/3-B**
891.44	+	-08

C. No. 891.4408

Title: Collections of Bengali literature dealing with literary themes.

Base No.		Collections Base No.		Table 3-A/3-C
891.44	+	-080	+	-17

C. No. 891.4408017

Title: Collection of 19th century Bengali literature.

Base No.		Collections base no.		notations 01-09 from Table 3-A/3-C		Period number
891.44	+	-080	+	0	+	4

C. No. 891.4408004

-09 HISTORY, DESCRIPTION, CRITICAL APPRISAL-PROCEDURE TO BE USED.

For practical purpose the notation -09 may be divided in the following manner:

I. By specific period
II. By additional elements enumerated in Table 3-A (Ed. 19) /3-C (Ed. 20)

I. BY SPECIFIC PERIOD

The provisions and the instructions to add -09 notation from period table are one and the same in both the editions. The instruction is given in the following manner:

-09001-09009 Literature from specific periods
Add to -0900 the notation from the period table for the specific literature in 810-890.

Practice-steps to be used

1a. Write the base number for specific literature as provided in 810-890;

2b. add -0900 to the base number as is given for -09 in Table 3/3-B;

3c. then add specific period number as provided in period table under the specific literature.

Examples:

Title: History and description of Marathi literature upto 1947

Base No.		-09 Base No.		Period Number as under 891.4
891.46	+	-0900	+	7

C. No. 891.4609007

Title: A collected biography of Marathi authors upto 1947

C. No. 891.4609007

II. BY ADDITIONAL ELEMENTS

Table 3-A of Edition 19 and Table 3-C of Edition 20 enumerate one and the same subdivisions. These subdivisions may also be used through -09 to provide additional elements in the specific literature. Following procedure is to be used to add notation from Table 3-A/3-C through -09.

IIa. write the base number of the specific literature as provided in 810-890;

IIb. add to base number -09 Table 3(Ed. 19), Table 3-B (Ed. 20) wherein the instruction under -091-099 Literature displaying specific features:- Add to -09 notation 1-9 from Table 3-A/3-C is given.

IIIc. then add notation from Table 3-A/3-C.

Examples:

Title: Critical appraisal of Sanskrit literature displaying romanticism

Base No.		Critical App Table 3/3-B		Table 3-A/3-C
891.2	+	-09	+	-145

C. No. 891.209145

Title: Collected biography of Sanskrit literary authors dealing with social themes

Base No.		Biography Table 3/3-B		Table 3-A/3-C
891.2	+	-09	+	-355

C. No. 891.209355

COLLECTED WORKS RESTRICTED TO ONE SPECIFIC FORM

To classify works by or about more than one author written in one specific form i.e. in poetry or drama or fiction etc. three different combinations are provided. DDC permits to add to specific form the following:

A. **First Combination**

Specific form + -001-009 Standard subdivisions; Collections; History, description...+ Table 3-A (Ed. 19) /Table 3-C (Ed. 20) Additional notation for literature;

Or

B. **Second Combination**

Specific form + Specific period + Table 3-A(Ed. 19)/Table 3-C(Ed. 20) Additional notation for literature;

Or

C. **Third Combination:**

Specific form + Specific scopes, kinds, types + Table 3-A(Ed. 19)/Table 3-C(Ed. 20) - Additional notation for literature.

A. WORKS RELATED TO MORE THAN ONE PERIOD

Specific form + 001-009 Standard Subdivisions; Collections; history, description... + Table 3-A(Ed. 19)/Table 3-C(Ed. 20) - Additional notation for literature:

The procedure to add above notation is similar in Editions 19 and 20. The minor difference in regard to instruction and enumeration in both these editions is as follows:

Edition 19: The notation -001-009 SS, Collections, history, etc., are enumerated under - 1 Poetry e.g.:

	-1001-1007	Standard subdivisions
Table 3	-1008	Collections...
	-1009	History...

and under -1008 and -1009 the instruction to add notation 1-9 from Table 3-A is provided. Under all other forms 2-8 instruction is provided directing the classifier to add numbers following -100 in -1001-1009. In other words to add notations of Table 3-A to forms 2-8 help of the instruction provided under -1008 and -1009 is required.

Edition 20

Whereas in Edition 20 no such enumeration is available under -1 Poetry. All the forms -1-8 are given uniform treatment by directing to add the notations of Table 3-C as per instruction given under -1-8 Specific forms on pages 398-399.

PRACTICE–STEPS TO BE USED

A1. write the base number for specific literature from the Schedules as is given in 810-890.

A2. to this add notation -001-009 SS, Collection, history...from Table 3(Ed. 19)/Table 3-B(Ed. 20);

A3. if the notation is -08 collections or -09 History ... then follow the instructions given under:

Ed. 19	-1008 and -1009	in Poetry as well as in different forms under the heading Standard subdivisions (Table 3)
Ed. 20	-1-8 Specific forms	(Pages 398-399) (Table 3B)

A4. then add required notation from Table 3-A(Ed. 19)/Table 3-C(Ed. 20).

Examples:

Title: Collections of Punjabi drama covering different periods displaying comedy

Edition 19: Table 3

-2 Drama

-2001-2009	Standard subdivisions Add -200 the numbers following -100 in -1001-1009
-1008	Collections ... Add to -10080 notations 1-9 from Table 3-A
-17	Comedy (Table 3-A)

Edition 20: Table 3-B

-2	Drama
-2001-2008	Standard subdivisions... Add to -200 as instructed under -1-8
-801-809	Collections... Add to 80 notation 1-9 from Table 3-C

Editions 19 + 20:

Punjabi language Base No.		**drama Base No.**		**Collection Base No.**		**Notation from Table 3-A/3-C**
891.42	+	-200	+	-80	+	17

C. No. 891.422008017

This clearly indicates that there is no difference in Editions 19 and 20 in building number for documents displaying specific forms and additional elements enumerated in Table 3-A/3-C.

B. WORKS RELATED TO SPECIFIC PERIOD

Specific form + Specific period + Table 3-A(Ed. 19)/Table 3-C(Ed. 20) - Additional notation for literature:

The procedure is similar in both the editions.

The necessary instructions to add specific period number and additional notation for literature is provided under each form e.g.:

Edition 19: Table 3

-11-19 Poetry of specific periods

Add to -1 the notation from period table for the specific literature; then to the result add the numbers following -10 in -1001-1009.

Edition 20: Table 3-B

-11-19 Poetry of specific periods

Add to -1 the notations from the period table for the specific literature in 810-890; then add 0 to the result add further as instructed under 1-8.

Example:

Title: Collections on 19th century Punjabi poetry displaying comedy

Editions 19 + 20:

Punjabi lang. Base No.		**Poetry Base No.**		**Period No. as under 891.4**		**Collections Base No.**		**Comedy Table 3-A/3-C**
891.42	+	-1	+	4	+	-080	+	17

C. No. 891.421408017

PRACTICE-STEPS TO BE USED

B1. write base number for specific literature from the Schedules in 810-890;

B2. to this add specific form number from Table 3(Ed. 19)/ Table 3-B(Ed. 20);

B3. then add number for specific period as provided for specific literature in 810-890;

B4. if desired, then add numbers following -10 in -1001-1009 and then add further as instructed under -1008 and -1009 (Edition 19);

Add 0 and to the result add further as instructed under 1-8 specific forms (Edition 20).

Example:

Title: Collections on 19th century Hindi poetry dealing with religious concepts

Hindi lang. Base No.		Poetry Table 3/3-B		Period No. as under 891.4
891.43	+	-1	+	4

Ed. 19 then to the result add numbers following -10 in -1001-1009. It means the required number would be - 1008 Collection...

Add to -10080 notations 1-9 from 3-A

Table 3-A 382 Religious concepts

i.e. [-10]080 + 382

C. NO. 891.4314080382

Ed. 20 then add 0 and to the result add further as instructed under 1-8 Specific forms

... 801-809 Collection displaying...

Add to 80 notation 1-9 from Table 3-C

Table 3-C 382 Religious concepts

i.e. 0 + 80 + 382

C. No. 891.4314080382

This clearly indicates that the difference in Editions 19 and 20 is in the instruction only. However, the procedure and result is the same.

If no Period Table

If there is no period table for the specific literature, add nothing to the form and the class number upto form be treated as complete.

C. SPECIFIC TYPES, KINDS AND SCOPE OF FORMS

Specific form + kinds, scope + Table 3-A (Edition 19) /Table 3-C (Edition 20) - Additional notation for literatures:

* Square brackets are used in all the examples to indicate the numbers following i.e. numbers which are not to be added.

In both the editions readymade numbers are enumerated for different kinds and scope of specific forms. To these notations from Table 3-A/3-C may be added as per instruction given under -1-8 Specific form (Ed. 19) and -102-108 Specific kinds of Poetry (Ed. 20). Under which the instruction states 'add to notation for each term identified by * (asterisk) as follow:

01-07 Standard subdivisions

08 Collections

Add to -08 notation...from Table 3-A/Table 3-C

09 History...

Add to -09 notation...from Table 3-A/Table 3-C

PRACTICE-STEPS TO BE USED

C1. write base number for specific literature from the Schedules 810-890;

C2. add to this number from Table 3/Table 3-B the enumerated number for kind, scope from the required form, e.g. -102 dramatic poetry;

C3. if the term for kind etc. is identified by * (asterisk) then add -08 or -09;

C4. then add notation from Table 3-A (Ed. 19) Table 3-C (Ed. 20)

Examples:

Title: Collections of Hindi short stories dealing with places

-301 *Short stories

Base No.		Form		Collection		Table 3-A/3-C
891.43	+	-301	+	-08	+	32

C. No. 891.433010832

Title: Critical appraisal of Hindi dramatic poetry of 19th Century

-102 *Dramatic

Base No. Lang.		Form Kind		Critical App		Table 3-A/3-C		period
891.43	+	-102	+	-09	+	-0	+	4

C. No. 891.431020904

LITERATURE IN MORE THAN ONE LANGUAGE

Literary works dealing with literature in general or related to more than one language are to be classed under Main Class 800 Literature itself or its subdivisions from 801-809. The class numbers 801-809 are divided into three main subdivisions:

801-807	*Standard subdivisions*
808	Rhetoric and collections of literary texts from more than one literature
809	History, description, critical appraisal of more than one literature

801-807 STANDARD SUBDIVISIONS

801 Philosophy and theory has been further subdivided to cover specific concepts like value, influence, psychology, history, techniques and theory of literary criticism. The classifier should note that DDC has specifically instructed under 809 to 'Class theory, technique, history of literary criticism in 801.95' and so documents dealing with theory, technique and history of literary criticism should be classed in 801.95 and not in 809. The class number 801.95 has been further subdivided on the basis of specific literary forms.

Examples:

Title: History of literary criticism upto early 20 century

801.95 Criticism
Theory, technique, history

.9501-.9509 Standard subdivisions

-09042 1920-1930 (Table 1)

C. No. 801.9509042

808 RHETORIC AND COLLECTIONS

Works on the art of speaking or writing in an impressive and effective style and collections of literary texts from more than one literatures are subdivided in the following manner:

808.001–009 Standard subdivisions of rhetoric

Standard subdivisions from Table 1 are to be added with works on rhetoric using two zeros, e.g.:

Title: Smith, Robert W. Art of rhetoric in Alexandria: Its theory and practice in ancient world

808	Rhetoric and collections
.001-.009	Standard subdivisions of rhetoric
-01	Philosophy and Theory (Table 1)

C. NO. 808.001

808.02–.06 General topics in rhetoric

This covers techniques of writing editorial, writing for publications and rhetoric in specific languages using notations of Table 6 Languages, as well as subdivision from 808.1-808.7 e.g.:

Title: Literature for learning Hindi rhetoric.

808	Rhetoric and collections
.04	Rhetoric is specific language
.043-.049	In other languages
	Add to base number 808.04 notations
	3-9 from Table 6
-9143	Hindi (Table 6)

Base No.		Table 6
808.04	+	-91431

C. NO. 808.0491431

Title: Art of writing poetry for children

808.06	Rhetoric of specific kinds of composition
.068	Children's literature

.0681-.0687 Specific literary forms

Add to base number 808.068 the numbers following 808 in 808.1-808.7

808.1 Rhetoric of poetry

Base No.		**Add numbers following 808**
808.068	+	[808.]1

C. No. 808.0681

808.1-.7 Rhetoric in specific literary forms are to be subdivided on the basis of the notations of Table 3 and its supplementaries e.g.:

Title: Art of writing drama for radio and television

808.2 Rhetoric of drama

Add to 808.2 numbers following -20 in notation 202–205 from Table 3 (Ed. 19)/Table 3-B (Ed. 20)

[-20]2 For radio and television

Base No.		**Table 3/3-B Numbers following -20**
808.2	+	[-20]2

C. NO. 808.22

808.8 COLLECTIONS FROM MORE THAN ONE LITERATURE

This again is subdivided on the basis of specific periods, specific features, specific forms and specific kinds of persons. For subdividing all these concepts the classifier is instructed to add historical periods from Standard subdivisions and notations from Table 3 and its supplementaries, e.g.:

Title: Collections of 20th century literature

808.8001-.8005 Collections from specific periods

Add to base numbers 808.800 the numbers following -090 in notation 0901-0905 from Table 1

Base No.		Period (Table 1)
808.800	+	[-090]4

C. No. 808.8004

Title: Collections of literature in varied languages by Indians

808.89 Collections for and by specific kinds of persons

Add to base number 808.89 notation 8-9 from Table 3-A (Ed. 19)/Table 3-C (Ed. 20)

Table 3-A
Table 3-C -8 Literature for and by Racial, ethnic...

Add to -8 notation 08-33 from Table 5

Table 5 -91411 Indians

Base No.		Table 3-A/3-C		Table 5
808.89	+	-8	+	-91411

C. No. 808.89891411

809 HISTORY, DESCRIPTION, CRITICAL APPRAISAL OF MORE THAN ONE LITERATURE

809.1-.7 Literature in specific forms

Instead of adding notations of Table 3 and its supplementaries directly to 809, the classifier is required to add number following 808.81–808.87 thereby saving unnecessary repetition of enumeration and instruction under each form e.g.:

Title: History and description of Western fiction

809.1-.7 Literature in specific forms

Add to base number 809 numbers following 808 in 808.81-808.87, i.e.

808.83 Collections of fiction

808.831–838 Specific scopes and types

Add to base number 808.83 the numbers following -30 in 301-308 from Table 3 (Ed. 19)/Table 3-B (Ed. 20), i.e.

[-30]874 Western fiction

Base No.		Nos. following 808		Table 3/3-B Nos. following -30
809	+	[808]83	+	[-30]874

C. NO. 809.83874

809.8 Literature for and by specific kinds of persons

The various types of literature for and by specific kinds of persons may be subdivided on the basis of notations from Table 3-A/3-C, Table 5 and the class numbers of the Schedules from 001-999.

Examples:

Title: Literature by Tibetans

809.889 Other

Add to base number 809.889 numbers following -9 in notation 91-99 from Table 5

-954 Tibetans

Base No.		Table 5 nos. following 9
809.889	+	[-9]54

C. No. 809.88954

Title: Appraisal of literary works in natural sciences

809.935 Literature emphasising subjects

Add to base number 809.935 notation 001-999

500 Natural sciences

Base No.		Add from 001-999
809.935	+	5[00]

C. No. 809.9355

OPTIONS

The following options are permitted to the classifier when local emphasis is required with the literature of the languages:

1. To give local emphasis and a shorter number other than American literature in English, class it in 810 e.g. Hindi literature and class American literature in English literature in 820;
2. To give preferred treatment by placing before 810 through use of letter or other symbol, e.g., 8HO Hindi literature. Base number for this would be 8H;
3. Two different methods may be used to provide local emphasis where two or more countries share the same language. These are:

   3.1 *By using initial letters* : For example, those countries which share English language may distinguish the English language literature by using initial letters of that particular country, e.g.:

Literature of England	E 820
Literature of India	In 820
Literature of Scotland	S 820

   3.2 Use of the special number designated for literature of those countries that are not preferred, e.g.:

If the classifier does not want to use the above methods (options 1 to 3.1), he may use the class number specially provided by DDC for literatures of those countries which are not preferred, e.g.:

810 American Literature in English

819 American Literature in English not requiring local emphasis

(Class here English language literatures of specific American countries than the countries requiring local emphasis, e.g. libraries emphasising United States literature may class here Canadian literature and libraries emphasising Canadian literature may class here United States literature...)

.1 Canada

.2 United States

.3 Mexico

OPTIONAL PERIOD NUMBERS

If the classifier has used either of the above methods, in that case he has to use the period table also accordingly, i.e., classifier has to use only that period table which is provided for that particular country. For instance, under 820 Literatures of English and Anglo-Saxon languages the following period tables are provided:

Period Tables for English

For African countries
For Asian countries
For Australia
For Great Britain
For Ireland
For New Zealand
For South Africa

The classifier has to use the above methods together with period table in the following manner:

Title: Later 20th century drama in English by Indian authors

	First Method
	822 English drama
	Period Table for Asian countries
	3 Later 20th Century 1947-
C. No.	In 822.3
	Second Method
828	English miscellaneous writings
.99	English-language literature not requiring local emphasis
.9935	*India

(*Add to base number as instructed under 810-890)
(through this instruction notations of Table 3 may be used)

-2	Drama
-21-29	Drama of specific periods Add to -2 the notation from the period table for the specific literature

820	Literatures of English
	Period Tables for English
	For Asian countries
3	Later 20th century 1947.

Base No.		Drama		Period Table
828.9935	+	-2	+	3

C. No. 828.993523

More than one period tables have been provided under English language to facilitate the use of above two methods. However, DDC makes it very clear that if none of the two methods is used for differentiating or distinguishing the literatures, then assign period numbers for literature of Great Britain only. That is the classifier should use period table of that country only to which the language is basically related.

4. The classifier may classify works by and about Shakespeare or other specific author according to Table 3/3-A or according to special table provided under 822.33 which states 'subarrange works about and by Shakespeare according to the following table, which may be adapted for use with any specific author'.

Practical Problems

1. Paradise Lost by John Milton (1604-1674).
2. My Story: An Autobiography of Kamla Das, an 20th century English fiction writer.
3. Biography of 19th century Gujarati poets.
4. Critical appraisal of Marathi poems having historical and political themes from 1648-1845.
5. An anthology of old Persian literature.
6. Collections of Dutch language historical drama.
7. History and description of Hindi literature by rural authors.
8. Complete works of Shakespeare with notes.
9. Technical writings in Russian language.

10. Polish poetry of golden period.
11. An art of story telling.
12. Collections of speeches dealing with nationalism.
13. Burmese fiction about mythological persons.
14. Collections of German narrative poetry.
15. Description of Italian essays of renaissance period.

Solutions :

1. 821.4
2. 823.91
3. 891.4714
4. 891.461309358
5. 891.5108
6. 839.312051408
7. 891.430991734
8. 822.33J
9. 808.66609171
10. 891.8513
11. 808.543
12. 808.859358
13. 895.83009351
14. 831.0308
15. 854.209

VI

TABLE 4
SUBDIVISIONS OF INDIVIDUAL LANGUAGES

Table 4 is specifically designed to enumerate linguistic elements required by individual languages provided under 420-490 in the Schedules. The general instruction to add notation of Table 4 is given under 420-490 Specific languages, which states 'Except for additions, changes, deletions, exceptions shown under specific entries, add to base number for each language identified by * notation 01-86 from Table 4'. This makes quite clear that before adding notation of Table 4 to a language enumerated in 420-490, the classifier is required to verify whether or not the specific language is identified by *(asterisk). In Edition 20 †(dagger) is also used for this purpose.

PRACTICE-STEPS TO BE USED

1. write the base number of the specific language as given in 420-490;
2. verify if the language is identified by *(asterisk) or †(dagger);

If Yes

3. then add to the base number the required notation from Table 4.

Examples:

Title: Grammatical sketch of Dard languages

491.499 Dard languages
Examples, Kashmiri...

C. No. 491.499

As the language is not identified by *the notation of Table 4 can not be added to it.

Title: Amrit Madhav Ghatage, Ed. - Phonemic and morphonic frequencies in Hindi

491.43 Western Hindi languages * Hindi
Base number for Hindi 491.43

-5 Structural system (Grammar) of the standard form of the language.
Class here comprehensive works on morphology, syntax and phonology (Table 4)

Base No.		**Table 4**
491.43	+	-5

C. No. 491.435

-2 ETYMOLOGY OF THE STANDARD FORM OF THE LANGUAGE

-24 Foreign elements

The term etymology may be defined as the 'Science or investigation of the derivation and original significance of words'. It covers the origin and development of a linguistic form as shown by determining its basic elements, discovering its earliest known use, recording changes in its form and meaning[1]. The term foreign elements in a language, therefore, indicates the use of such words in the language which belong originally to another language. Such works are to be classified using the notation -24 Foreign elements.

PRACTICE-STEPS TO BE USED:

1. write base number of the specific language under study from 420-490;
2. add to the base number notation -24 from Table 4;
3. then add from Table 6 the number for the language whose words are used in the above specific language.

Examples:

Title: Use of English Words in Hindi language

491.43 Western Hindi languages *Hindi

1. Webster's II New Riverside University Dictionary.

Base number for Hindi 491.43

-24 Foreign elements (Table 4)

Add to -24 notation 1-9 from Table 6.

-21 English (Table 6)

Base No.		Table 4		Table 6
491.43	+	-24	+	-21

C. NO. 491.432421

-3 DICTIONARIES OF THE STANDARD FORM OF THE LANGUAGE

A dictionary is a book containing the words of a language or the terms of a specific subject arranged alphabetically. It provides meaning of the words or terms, their etymology, pronunciation, etc.

-31 Specialised Dictionaries

Examples: Dictionaries of abbreviations, acronyms, synonyms, antonyms, and homonyms...

Examples:

Title: Webster's new dictionary of synonyms. Springfield, Massachusetts, 1968

420 *English and Anglo-Saxon languages

Table 4 -3 Dictionaries...

-31 Specialised dictionaries

Base No.		Table 4
42	+	-31

C. No. 423.1

Title: Allen, E.F. Dictionary of abbreviations and symbols N.Y. 1946

420 *English and Anglo-Saxon languages

Base number for English 42

Table 4 -3 Dictionaries...
-31 Specialised dictionaries

Base No.		Table 4
42	+	-31

C. No. 423.1

LANGUAGE DICTIONARIES

The class numbers for dictionaries of standard form of the languages in 420-480 have already been enumerated by DDC and so there is no need of using -3 from Table 4 with these languages. However, languages enumerated under 490 have to take help of Table 4 for this purpose.

Examples:

Title: Yeshwant Ramkrishna Date, Ed., Maharashtra Shabdakosh. 4 Vols. 1932-1937.

491.46 *Marathi
-3 Dictionaries of the standard form of the language (Table 4)

Base No.		Table 4
491.46	+	-3

C. No. 491.463

Title: Bengali Shabdkosh. 2 vols.

Base No.		Table 4
491.44	+	-3

C. No. 491.443

-32-39 BILINGUAL DICTIONARIES

Bilingual dictionary means a dictionary giving equivalent words in two different languages. It provides translations of words or terms of a language into another or explaining the words or terms of the two languages in-terse. For example, in English-

Hindi dictionary: the words of English are translated into Hindi i.e., providing equivalent words in Hindi.

RULES TO DETERMINE FIRST AND SECOND LANGUAGE IN A BILINGUAL DICTIONARY

As a bilingual dictionary deals with two specific languages, the number for both languages need to be provided in the class number of a bilingual dictionary. The DDC instructs to use number for one language from 420-490 and for another from Table 6. The classifier is, therefore, required not to classify a bilingual dictionary on the basis of the title of such a dictionary. As DDC has laid down definite guide-lines to select, which should be the first or second language in the class number. Such guide-lines are provided under -32-39 Bilingual dictionaries in Table 4. The rules are as follows:

Rule 1: Class a bilingual dictionary with the language in which it will be more useful

The usefulness of the language depends on the library in which the bilingual dictionary is being classified. For instance, for libraries of Hindi speaking regions, English will be useful language. Similarly, most libraries in English-speaking regions will find English-German dictionaries most useful classed with German. In simple words, a language which is difficult or less known by the readers of library will be termed as useful language.

Examples:

Title: Raghuvira, Comprehensive English-Hindi Dictionary, Nagpur 1955.

420	English and Anglo-Saxon languages Base number for English 42
-3	Dictionaries...(Table 4)
-32-39	Bilingual dictionaries Add to -3 notation 2-9 from Table 6
-91431	Standard Hindi (Table 6)

Base No.		**Table 4**		**Table 6**
42	+	-3	+	-91431

C. No. 423.91431

Note : Here English language has been treated as useful language because in the libraries of Hindi speaking regions English language will be treated as less known language.

Rule 2 : If classification with either language is equally useful, class with the language coming later in the sequence 420-490

The first language, under which the dictionary will be classed, according to this rule will be the language which is enumerated later in the sequence 420-490, e.g. French-Spanish dictionary. The class number for French language is 440 and for Spanish language is 460 in the Schedules. It means Spanish language coming after French language in the sequence 420-490 will be the first language.

Examples:

Title: Spanish-Latin Dictionary

	470	*Italic languages Latin Base number for Latin: 47
Table 4	-3	Dictionaries....
	-32-39	Bilingual dictionaries Add to -3 notation 2-9 from Table 6
	-61	Spanish (Table 6)

Base No.		**Table 4**		**Table 6**
47	+	-3	+	-61

C. No. 473.61

Note : Here 470 Latin language is enumerated after 461 Spanish language in the sequence 420-490, so the dictionary will be classed under Latin.

SUBJECT DICTIONARIES

A subject dictionary is confined to a specific subject or several related subjects. It provides the meaning and use of the specialised or the technical terms of the subject. A subject dictionary is to be classed in the subject which it covers and the notation -03 Dictionary is to be added to it from Table 1 Standard subdivisions.

Examples:

Title: Thewlis J. Concise Dictionary of Physics and Related Terms, Oxford, 1973.

530	Physics
.01-.09	Standard subdivisions
-03	Dictionaries, encyclopaedias, concordances

Base No.		Table 1
530	+	-03

C. No. 530.03

Edition 19 : In 19th Edition -03 may be further sub-divided by language, i.e. the language of the dictionary e.g.

Table 1	-03	Dictionaries...
	-032-039	By language
		Add "Languages" notation 2-9 from Table 6 to base number -03
	-21	English (Table 6)

So the class number of the above dictionary according to 19th Edition will be:

Base No.		Table 1		Table 6
530	+	-03	+	-21

C. No. 530.0321

Edition 20 : This provision has been discontinued in Edition 20. So the class number for the above dictionary in Edition 20 would be: 530.03

-7 HISTORICAL AND GEOGRAPHICAL VARIATIONS

The notation -7 is used to indicate the historical, geographical and modern non-geographical variations among the standard form of languages. Therefore all the subdivisions enumerated from -1 to -5 and -8 of this Table are also to be classed under -7 when these indicate to historical, geographical and modern nongeographical variations.

A specific language may be distorted by mixing words of another foreign language in the standard form or the standard form has been twisted or modified in such way that it acquires a distinct style and way of speaking with altogether different meaning and grammatical characteristics. Such a language becomes the language of a particular geographical area or region where it is so spoken. To indicate such differences and geographical variations among the standard form of languages, subdivisions of -7 are also enumerated under some of the individual languages in 420-490 in the following manner:

Examples:

Title: A study of the dialects of Bari

457 Historical and geographical variations

.1-.7 Geographical variations in continental Italy

Add to 457 the numbers following 45 in notation 451-457 from Table 2

Table 2 -45751 Bari province
class here Bari

Base No.		**Nos. following -45 (Table 2)**
457	+	[-45]751

C. No. 457.751

Title: Grammatical characteristics of the dialects of Eastern Siberia

491.7 Russian

.774-.779 Geographical variations

Add to 491.77 notation 4-9 from Table 2

-575 Eastern Siberia (Table 2)

Base No.		**Table 2**
491.77	+	-575

C. No. 491.77575

–8 APPLIED LINGUISTICS

The various linguistic elements such as meaning, spelling, pronunciation, grammar etc. required to study, learn and use of language are enumerated under -8. The enumeration in both the Editions 19 and 20 is similar. The minor difference is in -802. Translation to and from languages, where instruction to add second language from Table 6 has been provided in Edition 20. This instruction is Not available in Edition 19.

Example:

Title: Translating from English into Hindi

Translating to Base No		Table 4		Translating from Table 6
491.43	+	-802	+	-21

C. No. 491.4380221 (Ed. 20)
C. No. 491.43802 (Ed. 19)

LEARNING A LANGUAGE

The subdivisions from -82 to -86 are specifically provided to classify such aids, readers, texts which help in learning, or increasing proficiency of poor readers or to practice in reading a language to those:

1. whose native language is different;
2. native speakers who are learning the acceptable patterns of their language.

Examples:

Title: Potapova, N. Learning Russian. Pt 1 (Presents fundamentals of Russian phonetics, elementary grammar and vocabulary for those who know English language)

491.7	East Slavic languages *Russian Base number for Russian 491.7
-82	Structural approach to expression (Table 4)
-824	For those whose native language is different Add to -824 notation 2-9 from Table 6
-21	English (Table 6)

Base No.		Table 4		Table 6
491.7	+	-824	+	-21

C. No. 491.782421

Title: Potapova, N. Russian, an elementary course (for those who know English language)

491.7 East Slaic languages 'Russian
Base number for Russian 491.7
-86 Readers
-864 *For those whose native language is different*
Add to -864 notation 2-9 from Table 6
-21 English (Table 6)

Base No.		Table 4		Table 6
491.7	+	-864	+	-21

C. No. 491.786421

Title: French language proficiency reader

Base No.		Table 4
44	+	-842

C. No. 448.42

READERS FOR NON-NATIVE SPEAKERS IN SPECIFIC SUBJECTS

In Edition 20 under the notations -864 the classifier is directed to *see in Manual T4 - 864 Vs. T1 - 011.* Wherein the following instruction for classifying documents relating 'readers for non - native speakers in specific subjects' is given:-

Such readers which help in instilling knowledge of the special vocabulary of a specific subject or discipline to those whose native language is different are to be classed as follows:

Title: Medical science reader in French for Spanish speaking people

Base No. language		Table 4 Base No.		Table 6 Native lang		Table 1 Spec. users		Table 7 Subject
44	+	-864	+	61	+	024	+	61

C. No. 448.646102461

It means readers for non-native speakers is to be classified in the language in which it is written.

However, works on the vocabulary of a specific subject or discipline not written from the point of view of non-native speakers are to be classed in the subject or discipline using notation -014 from Table 1. e.g.,

Title: Medical science reader

Base No.		Table 1
61	+	-014

C. No. 610.14

LINGUISTICS

The subdivisions enumerated from 401 to 419 in main class 400 are more or less analogus to the subdivisions included in Table 4. That is why the notations of Table 4 are not required by these subdivisions. However, such concepts which need to be subdivide or sharpen or individualise, the help of other Tables may be taken, e.g.:

Title: Sanskrit-German-Latin Dictionary having definitions in Sanskrit only

	413	Dictionaries
In Edition 20 only	413.2-.9	Polyglot dictionaries with entry words of definitions in only one language Add to base number 413 notation 2-9 from Table 6
	-912	Sanskrit (Table 6)

C. No. 413.912

This provision is not available in Edition 19.

THREE OR MORE LANGUAGES

The classifier should also note that a book dealing with the comparison of three or more languages would be classed on the basis of the following rules:

Rule 1: Class a comparison of three or more languages in the most specific number that will contain them all, e.g.:

Title: **Comparison of Swedish, Danish and German grammar;**

C. No. 430

Rule 2: If there is no number that will contain all the languages then class such a work in 410, e.g.:

Title: **Comparison of Russian, German and Latin Grammar.**

C. No. 415

Rule 3: Class a comparison of two languages with the language requiring local emphasis (usually the language that is less common in the particular library) e.g.:

Title: **Comparison of Sanskrit and Russian alphabets**

C. No. 491.711 (in India)

but

491.211 (in Russia)

Rule 3-A However, if no emphasis is required, class the work with the language coming later in Table 6.

Rule 4: Class a language of a specific discipline or subject with the discipline or subject using notation 014 from Table 1, e.g.:

Title: A study of the terminology used in Library and Information Science

C. No. 020.14

OPTIONS

If desired, the classifier may opt for one of the following two options to give preferred treatment or shorter number to a specific language.

Option A: To give local emphasis and a shorter number to a specific language class in 410, add to base number 41 as instructed under 420-490, e.g.:

41 Hindi language

413 Hindi language dictionary

If this option is opted then class 410 Linguistics in 400 and subdivisions of Linguistics in 401-409. Then the Standard subdivisions of language and linguistics would be classed in 400.1-400.9

Option B: To give local emphasis and a shorter number to a specific language place it first by use of a letter or other symbol, e.g.:

4HO Hindi language

The base number for this would be 4H. After this add notation from Table 4 e.g.:

4H3 Hindi language dictionary

The place of this number would be preceding to 420.

With the help of these two options the classifier may use one of the three numbers assigned to the specific language as per local needs of the library:

410 or 4HO or 491.43 Hindi language

Option C: If desired, for any group of languages, add 04 to the base number and then add notation 01-86 from Table 4, e.g.:

496.39045 Grammar of Bantu languages.

Practical Problems

1. Old Portuguese.
2. Comparative study of Hebrew, Aramaic and modern Arabic languages.
3. Dictionary of French homonyms.
4. French abbreviations.
5. Works on Indo-European languages.
6. How a child learns a language from his parents.
7. English language proficiency readers.
8. Moravian dialetcs.
9. Arabic Russian dictionary.
10. A study of the structural system of Latin American dialects.
11. Discussions on lingua francas.
12. Reverse acronyms and initialisms dictionary.
13. A study of phonetic development of words.
14. French, German and Russian dictionary.

Solutions:

1. 469.701
2. 492
3. 443.1
4. 441
5. 410
6. 401.93
7. 428.42
8. 491.87

9. 492.739171
10. 467.98
11. 401
12. 423.1
13. 414
14. 413.

VII

TABLE 5
RACIAL, ETHNIC, NATIONAL GROUPS

Table 5 provides notations for basic races, ethnic and national groups. Basic races–as Negro race, ethnic groups as - Sinhalese; national group as Indian, or Japanese, etc. All the divisions which are based on languages are similar in Table 5 and Table 6 Languages having the same sequence as is provided in 420-490 specific languages. However, Table 5 is necessary: firstly it refers to the groups of people and secondly the group of people may speak common language yet may belong to different ethnic or cultural groups or nationality.

ENUMERATION IN EDITION 19 AND 20

There is no difference in Editions 19 and 20 in so far as the enumeration of concepts and use of Table 7 is concerned. However, in Edition 20 few new numbers are interpolated to individualise some races and categories of people, e.g.:

914122	Pakistanis	Edition 19 provides only broad numbers
91593	Afghans (Pashtun)	
94811	Tamil	
94812	Malayalis	
94814	Kanarese (Kannada)	

Similarly 971-979 are all new numbers for individualising North American native races and 982-984 for individualising South American native races.

POINTS TO NOTE

Before adding the notation of Table 5, the classifier is required to note the following two points:

1. CITATION ORDER

That the general citation order followed in Table 5 is

(11) Ethnic group
(12) Nationality
(13) Basic races

2. ORDER OF PRECEDENCE

If the documents deal with any of the two or all three categories, then the following guidelines are to be followed for giving priority to their notation;

(21) In the Introduction of Table 5 of Edition 20 the classifier has been clearly instructed to give precedence first to ethnic group, second to nationality and last to basic races.

However, the classifier should note that there are some exception to this rule wherein this general preferred citation has been changed,

Example

-11 Canadian
-112 of British origin
-114 of French origin

Here the priority is given to nationality and second place to ethnic group.

(22) In case of minority ethnic group vis-a-vis nationality, priority would be given to ethnic group, e.g.,

Canadian citizens who are ethnic Japanese would be classed;

-956 Japanese (Table 5)
-0 Connecting symbol
-71 Canada (Table 2)
-956071

(23) If this ethnic group which is citizen of a particular

country moves to another country it would be classed in the following manner :

Canadian citizens who are ethnic Japanese move to United States

-956	Japanese (Table 5)
-0	Connecting symbol
-73	United States (Table 2)
-956073	

(24) However, if the ethnic group is also viewed as the national group and it moves to another country it would be classed:

Japanese citizens who are ethnic Japanese move to United States

-956	Japanese
-0	Connecting symbol
-73	United States (Table 2)
-956073	

(25) When choosing between two national groups give precedence to the former or ancestral national group, e.g.:

People from Japan who have become citizens of United States

-956	Japanese (Table 5)
-0	Connecting symbol
-73	U.S.A. (Table 2)
-956073	

3. VERIFY ALSO INSTRUCTIONS GIVEN UNDER SPECIFIC NUMBERS

The classifier is also required to verify the instructions given under various specific numbers before adding notation of Table 5 e.g.:

91418	Bhutanese
	Class the Bhutia as an ethnic group in -954
-9144	Bengali

Class the Bengali of Bangladesh in -914126

-954 Tibetans

Class here the Bhutia as an ethnic group.

PRACTICAL APPLICATIONS

The notation of Table 5 may be added to the class numbers of specific subjects from the Schedules in the following ways;

1. Through the instructions provided under specific class number for adding notation of Table 5
2. Through Table 1 Standard subdivisions -089

1. THROUGH INSTRUCTION - PROVIDED UNDER THE SPECIFIC SUBJECTS

For all those subjects wherein DDC desires to provide racial, ethnic, national element, the instruction to add notation from Table 5 is provided under such subjects.

PRACTICE-STEPS TO BE USED

1. Write the base number for the specific subject as provided in the instruction;
2. add to it required notation from Table 5.

Examples:

Title: Cultural ethnology of North American native races

Base No.		**Table 5**
572.8	+	-97

C. No. 572.897

Title: Social status of Tibetans

Base No.		**Table 5**
305.8	+	-954

C. No. 305.8954

2. USE OF TABLE 5 THROUGH NOTATION -089 OF TABLE 1

Standard Subdivisions

The notation of Table 5 may be used freely through Standard

subdivision - 089 with all such class numbers of the schedules wherein no instruction to add notation from Table 5 is provided. Thereby the classifier may use these notations as per requirements of the documents.

CAUTION

The classifier should keep in mind that basically - 089 is a notation of Table 1 Standard Subdivisions. Therefore, while using notations of Table 5 through the notation - 089, he should follow all the rules applicable to Standard Subdivisions. As and when the notations of Table 5 are used through the notation - 089 of S.S., its imperative for the classifier to read instruction's note given under the class numbers in the Schedules, in regard to the use of standard subdivisions. For example the instruction to use two or more zeros for Standard Subdivisions.

PRACTICE-STEPS TO BE USED

1. write the base number for the specific subject from the schedules with which the notation of Table 5 is required i.e. remove zero or zeros if the class number ends with zero or zeros;
2. verify if the instruction for the use of Standard subdivisions is provided;
3. if yes, then add zero or zeros as per instruction to -089 before adding it to the base number, if not, then add directly;
4. then add notation from Table 5 as per instruction given under the SS notation-089 Racial, ethnic, national groups.

Title: Faith on astrological symbolism among Indians

133.5 Astrological symbolism.

-089 Racial, ethnic, national groups (Table 1)

Add to base number -089 notation 03-99 from Table 5

-91411 Indians (Table 5)

C. No. 133.508991411

Title: Folkways of Tibetans

390	Folkways
	Use 390.001-390.009 for Standard subdivisions
-089	Racial, ethnic...(Table 1)
-954	Tibetans (Table 5)

C. No. 390.0089954

USE OF TABLE 5 TOGETHER WITH OTHER TABLES

1. TABLE 2 AREAS AND TABLE 5

There are two different provisions through which the notations of Table 5 and Table 2 may be used together.

A. Through (zero) as Connecting Symbol

The first method is described in the introduction of Table 5 itself wherein it is stated that 'Except where instructed otherwise, and unless it is redundant, add 0 to the number from this table and to the result add notation 1-9 from Table 2'. This enables the classifier to individualise the geographical element in the specific subject. As per this direction the sequence would be;

Specific subject + Table 5 + 0 + Table 2

Practice-steps to be used

(i) Write the base number of the required specific subject as is available in the Schedules;

(ii) add to it the notation from Table 5;

(iii) then add to it zero;

(iv) then add Areas notation from Table 2.

Although in Edition 19 under certain class numbers the instruction given for adding notation for Table 5 also repeats this direction to add 0 and then Areas notation after notation of Table 5. But in Edition 20 this has been rectified as no such repetition is found under these class numbers now.

Examples:

Title: Psychology of Indians living in Kuwait

155.8 Ethnopsychology and national psychology

.84 Specific racial, ethnic groups.

Add to base number 155.84 notation 01-99 from Table 5

-91411 Indians (Table 5)

add 0 then add notation 1-9 from Table 2

-5367 Kuwait (Table 2).

C. No. 155.849141105367

Title: How popular is Punjabi cookery in USA

641.592 Ethnic cookery

Add to base number 641.592 notation -03-99 from Table 5

-9142 Punjabis (Table 5)

add 0 then add notation 1-9 from Table 2

-73 USA (Table 2).

C. No. 641.5929142073

B. Through Areas Notation -174

This is a common method in DDC which is being used to facilitate the use of notations of two Tables. In Table 2 Areas the notation -174 has been allotted to specify regions where specific racial, ethnic, national groups predominate. The instruction under -174 permits to add notation from Table 5.

PRACTICE-STEPS TO BE USED

(i) write the base number for the specific subject as available in the Schedules;

(ii) add to this the Areas notation -174 from Table 2. But before adding the notation classifier has to verify if -174 is to be used directly on the basis of the instruction to add Areas or through -09 Standard subdivision;

(iii) then add required notation from Table 5.

Examples:

Title: Education of women in regions where Anglo-Indians predominate

376 Education of women

376.9 Historical, geographical....

Add to base number 376.9 notation...from Table 2

-174 Regions where...

Add to base number -174 notation -03-99 from Table 5 (Table 2)

-91411 Indians

Including Anglo-Indians (Table 5)

C. No. 376.917491411

2. TABLE 3 AND TABLE 5

3-A Ed. 19 / 3-C Ed. 20 -8 Literature for and by various specific racial, ethnic national groups.

Add to -8 notation 03-19 from Table 5

Examples:

Title: Collections of literature by Indians

808.89 Collections for and by specific kind of persons

Add to base number 808.89 notation 8-9 from Table 3-A/3-C

-8 Literature for and by (Table 3-A/3-C)

Add to -8...from Table 5

-91411 Indians (Table 5)

C. No. 808.89891411

OPTIONS

There are two options which the classifier may use to give local emphasis or a shorter number to a specific group.

A. To give local emphasis and a shorter number to a specific group, place it first by use of a letter or another symbol, e.g., Indians - I (preceding - 1)

B. To give local emphasis and a shorter number to a specific group class it in - 1 used for North American and class North Americans in -2.

PRACTICAL PROBLEMS

1. Punjabi folk songs.
2. Social study of Indians living in England.
3. Social problems of Tibetans living in India.
4. A study of family system and marriage among the Burmese.
5. A study of South Asian races.
6. Critical appraisal of Jewish literature.
7. World history of Afro-Americans.
8. Class struggle among Indians.
9. Biographies of the French.
10. Social status of Nepalese living in India.
11. Works on social behaviour of people of Indian origin living in Japan.
12. Causes of crimes in areas where gypsies predominate.

SOLUTIONS

1. 784.769142
2. 305.891411042
3. 305.8954054
4. 306.8089958
5. 572.8914
6. 809.88924
7. 909.0496073
8. 305.508991411
9. 920.009241
10. 305.891495054
11. 395.08991411052
12. 364.917491497

VIII

TABLE 6
LANGUAGES

The notation of Table 6 Languages to some extent correspond to specific languages numbers under 420-490 and 810-890 in the Schedules. In so far as the enumeration and use of the notations of Table 6 is concerned, there is no difference in Edition 20 and Edition 19.

PRACTICAL APPLICATIONS

Out of all the seven tables, the use of notations of Table 6 still are restricted by instructions, which are as follows :

1. Use of Table 6 through instructions provided in specific subjects, disciplines in the Schedules.
2. Use of Table 6 through instructions provided in notations of other tables.

1. INSTRUCTIONS PROVIDED IN THE SCHEDULES

The classifier may add notations of Table 6 to only those class numbers wherein necessary instruction in this regard is given.

Examples:

Title: General encyclopaedias written in Dutch language

030 General encyclopaedic works

033 In other Germanic languages

Add to base number 03 notation 31-394 from Table 6

-3931 Dutch (Table 6)

C. No. 033.931

Title: (a) Tamil folktales from Tamil speaking areas of the world

(b) Tamil folktales from Tamil Nadu.

398.2 Folk literature

.204 By language

Add to base number 398.204 notation 1-9 from Table 6; however class tales (folk literature) of specific language where that language predominates in 398.209

(a) **Base No.** **Table 6**

398.204 + 94811

C. No. 398.20494811

(b) **Base No.** **Table 2**

398.209 + -5482

C. No. 398.2095482

In Edition 20 the above instruction specifically directs that if folk literature relates to the area where that language predominates then the Areas number and not the language number be assigned. In Edition 19 this direction is given under 398.232.

400 LANGUAGE AND 800 LITERATURE

The instructions provided under 420-490 Specific languages and 810-890 Literature of specific languages, specifically directs the classifier to use notation from Table 6 only when so directed. Accordingly, this instruction is given under such languages for which broad number are provided in 420-490.

Examples:

Title: Egyptian languages

493 Non-Semitic Afro-Asian languages.

Add to 493 the numbers following -93 in notation 931-937 from Table 6

-931 Egyptians (Table 6)

Base No.		Table 6 Nos. following 93
493	+	[-93]1

C. No. 493.1

Title: Hoken language literature

897 Literatures of North American native language

Add to 897 the numbers following -97 in notation 971-979 from Table 6

-975 Hoken and Siohan languages

Including Yukin

Base No.		Table 6 Nos following -97
897	+	[-97]5

C. No. 897.5

2. INSTRUCTIONS IN OTHER TABLES

TABLE 1 STANDARD SUBDIVISIONS

-03 Dictionaries...

In Edition 19 the instruction to add languages notation from Table 6 was provided under -032-039. This enables to provide language number to subject dictionaries also, e.g.:

Title: Library and Information Science glossary in Hindi

020 Library and information Science

-03 Dictionaries] Table 1

-032-039 By Language]

Add language notation 2-9 from Table 6 to base number -03.

-91431 Hindi (Table 6)

C. No. 020.391431

In Edition 20 this provision has been discontinued.

TABLE 2 AREAS

The notation of Table 6 and Table 2 may be added:

(i) through instructions given in the Schedules

(ii) through Areas notation - 175

(i) Through instruction given in the Schedules:

For such subjects in the Schedules wherein both the areas and language elements are required to devise the class number, the instruction to add notation both from Table 2 and Table 6 has been given together with citation order.

Example :

Title: Tamil speaking people in Asia.

305.7 Language groups.

Add to base number 305.7 notation 1-9 from Table 6; then add 0 and to the result add notation 1-9 from Table 2.

-94811 Tamil (Table 6)

-5 Asia (Table 2)

Base No.		*Table 6*		Add		Table 2
305.7	+	-94811	+	0	+	-5

C. No. 305.79481105

(ii) Through Areas notation -175

In the introduction of Table 6 Languages it is indicated that through Areas notation -175 the notation of Table 6 may be used wherein instruction in this regard is given.

However, as the Areas notation may be used through the notation - 09 of Standard Subdivision Table 1, the classifier has therefore some autonomy to use the notations of Table 2 through - 175 as and when necessary.

Examples:

Title: Psychology of school children of areas where Maithili language predominates.

155.4 Child psychology

.424 Children six to eleven

-091 Treatment by areas, regions...(SS Table 1)

Add to base number -091 the numbers following -1 in -11-19 from Table 2.

-175 Regions where specific languages predominate (Table 2)

Add to base number -175 notation 1-9 from Table 6.

-91454 Maithili (Table 6)

Base No.		SS (Table 1)		Number following -1 (Table 2)		Table 6
155.424	+	-091	+	[-1]75	+	-91454

C. No. 155.4240917591454

Through Table 4 Subdivisions for Individual Languages:

Table 4 is meant specifically for individual languages enumerated in the Main Class 400 Languages from 420-490. As Table 6 enumerates more or less similar languages in 420-490, the notation of Table 6 is therefore used with Table 4 only when the specific subject requires two different languages simultaneously. In such cases the classifier is directed to use one language from the Schedules and another from Table 6 through Table 4.

Examples:

Title: Modern Greek reader for English speaking people

489.3 Modern Greek

-86 Readers (Table 4)

-864 For those whose native language is different.
Add to -864 notation 2-9 from Table 6

-21 English (Table 6)

Base No.		Table 4		Table 6
489.3	+	-864	+	-21

C. No. 489.386421

OPTIONS

This table also permits to use one of the following options

to comply with local needs of the library.

Option A: To give local emphasis and a shorter number to a specific language, place it first by use of a letter or symbol, e.g., Hindi language H (preceding 1).

Option B: To give local emphasis and a shorter number to a specific language class it in -1 and class Indo-European languages in -91.

DIRECTIONS

There are some specific directions which the classifier should keep in view while using notation of Table 6. These are :

(i) Unless there is specific provisions for old or middle form of a modern language, class these forms with the modern language;

(ii) Unless there is specific provisions for a dialect of a language, class the dialect with the language;

(iii) Unless there is specific provision for a pidgin or creole, class it with the source language from which more of its vocabulary comes than from its other source language(s).

Practical problems

1. A study of voting behaviour of areas where Urdu language predominates.
2. Bible in Hindi.
3. General serial publications written in Urdu language.
4. A study of French rhetoric through critical readings.
5. Bengali proverbs.
6. Social status of German speaking people in USA.
7. A collection of essays in Hindi.
8. Indonesian languages.
9. Translation of Talmudic literature in French.
10. Whitaker's Almanack.

Solutions

1. 324.917591439

2. 220.591431
3. 059.91439
4. 808.04417
5. 398.99144
6. 305.731073
7. 089.91431
8. 499.22
9. 296.120541
10. 032.02

IX

TABLE 7
GROUPS OF PERSONS

In Edition 19 Table 7 is termed as 'Persons' which in Edition 20 has been renamed as 'Groups of Persons'. However, the enumeration of concepts remains the same.

In a general way, the notation and concepts enumerated in Table 7 with some exceptions, have been based on the enumeration of main classes of the Schedules. For example subject specialists enumerated under -1 to 9 correspond to main classes 100 to 900 e.g.:

-1 Persons occupied with philosophy, psychology...
-2 Persons occupied with religion.
-3 Persons occupied with social sciences
-4 Persons occupied with linguistics

With the result it has added mnemonic quality to the notation of Table 7.

The notations of the Table 7 may be added to the class numbers of specific subjects enumerated in the Schedules in the following ways:

1. through the instructions provided under the specific subjects in the Schedule*
2. through Table 1 Standard subdivisions -024 and -088

1. THROUGH INSTRUCTION IN THE SCHEDULES

There are class numbers in the Schedules wherein the subject need additional element as is enumerated in Table 7. In such subjects DDC directs the classifier to use notations of Table 7 through the instructions provided under these class numbers.

---

* Square brackets are used in all examples to indicate numbers following i.e. numbers not to be added.

PRACTICE–STEPS TO BE USED

1. write the base number as provided in the instruction;
2. add to it required number from Table 7

Example:

Title: Ethics of hotel and motel keepers

174.9 Other profession and occupations

Add to base number 174.9 notation -09-99 from Table 7

-647 Hotel and motel keepers (Table 7)

C. No. 174.9647

Title: Reading and use of other information media by school children

Base No.		**Table 7**
028.53	+	[-05]44

C. No. 028.5344

2 USE OF TABLE 7 THROUGH TABLE 1 STANDARD SUBDIVISIONS

The classifier also may use notations of Table 7 through Table 1. Standard subdivisions -024 and -088 with all such specific subjects wherein no instruction is available for adding notations of Table 7.

PRACTICE–STEPS TO BE USED

1. write the base number for the specific subject with which the notations of Table 7 is required to be used, i.e. remove zero or zeros if the class number ends with zero or zeros;
2. verify if the instruction for the use of standard subdivisions is provided;
3. if yes - then add zeros as directed to -024 and -088 before adding the number to the class number of specific subject; otherwise add directly;
4. then add notation from Table 7 as per instruction given under -024 and -088 in Editions 19 and 20.

-24 WORKS FOR SPECIFIC TYPE OF USERS

Examples:

Title: Works on food and foodstuffs for old persons

641.3 Food

-024 Works for specific types of users (Table 1)

Add to base number -024 notation 03-99 from Table 7

-0565 Late adulthood (Table 7)

Base No.		Table 1		As per Inst.		Table 7
641.3	+	-024	+	0024	+	-0565

C. No. 641.300240565

Title: Works on manufacture of textiles and clothing for public entertainers

677 Textiles

Class here comprehensive works on manufacture of textiles and clothing

-024 Works for...(Table 1)

-791 Public performances (Table 7)

Base No.		Table 1		As per Inst.		Table 7
677	+	-024	+	0024	+	-791

C. No. 677.0024791

-88 SPECIFIC KINDS OF PERSONS

-088: In so far as Standard subdivisions -088 is concerned there are following modifications and additions in Edition 20.

1. In Edition 19 under the notation-088 Treatment among group of specific kinds of persons, the add instruction was used to add notation -04-99 from Table 7 and there was no enumeration under -088.

Whereas in Edition 20 the subdivisions enumerated in Edition 19 from -04 to -08 in Table 7 have been shifted to Table 1 under -08 History and description with respect to kinds of persons.

Meaning thereby, that those divisions which could be used in Edition 19 through -088, in Edition 20 may be used directly as Standard subdivisions.

2. In Table 7 the notation -06 is allotted to Persons by social and economic characteristics. In Edition 19 all the 26 subdivisions of -06 have been enumerated under -06 in Table 7 itself whereas in Edition 20 these have been shifted to Table 1 and under -06 the instruction 'Add to base number -06 the numbers following -086 in -0862-0869 from Table 1' is given. The 26 divisions have been increased to 32 in Edition 20.

3. Due to all these modifications and enumerations of subdivisions (formerly of Table 7) in Table 1, the notation -088 has been restricted to occupational and religious groups in Edition 20. The add instruction now given under -08809-08899 specific occupational and religious group in Table 1 is used to add notation -09-99 from Table 7 as notation -04-08 have been shifted to Table 1.

However, in so far as the use of all these subdivisions related to 'Persons' is concerned there is no change. In Edition 19 these could be used through -088 and in Edition 20 some may be used directly as standard subdivisions and remaining through -088.

Examples:

Title: Correspondence school and courses for farmers

Base No.		Table 1		Table 7
374.4	+	-088	+	-631

C. No. 374.4088631

USE OF NOTATIONS OF TABLE 7 TOGETHER WITH NOTATIONS OF OTHER TABLES

TABLE 2 - AREAS

In Table 2 the notation - 176 has been used to subdivide such areas which are dominated by people of specific religions. For this purpose the notation of Table 7 enumerated under -29

With other religions, have been used and specific instruction to add notation from Table 7 is given under -176 Regions where specific religions predominate. For areas predominated by Christian religion readymade class numbers are enumerated.

Example:

Title: A study of factors affecting social behaviour in areas where Bahai faith predominates

Base No.		Table 1		Table 2		Table 7
304	+	-09	+	-176	+	-2979

C. No. 304.091762979

TABLE 3. A/3-C ADDITIONAL ELEMENTS FOR SUBDIVISIONS FOR INDIVIDUAL LITERATURES

The Table 3-A (Edition 19) and 3-C (Edition 20) enumerate additional elements for individual literatures enumerated under 810-890 in the Schedules. In this Table under the notation -92 for and by persons of specific classes, the instruction is provided through which the groups of persons enumerated in Table 7 may be used with individual literatures, to indicate the specific group of persons for whom, by whom the literature is written. The add instruction is provided under -9204-9209 and -929.

Title: A collection of English fiction by lawyers

Base No.		Table 3/3-B		Table 3-A/3-C		Table 7
82	+	-30080	+	-92	+	-344

C. No. 823.008092344

Title: A collection of literature for historians

Base No		Table 3-A/3-C		Table 7
808.89	+	-92	+	-97 (Ed. 19)
		-929	+	[9]7 (Ed. 20)

C.No. 808.899297

DIRECTIONS

With regard to complex subjects the classifier is required to keep in view the following direction:

'Unless other instructions are given, class complex subjects with aspects in two or more subdivisions of this Table in the number coming *last* in the table', e.g.:

Retired lower middle class females

Class in:

-0696 Retired persons

and not in -042 female, or -0623 lower middle classed.

Practical problems

1. Books on gardening for Women.
2. Need of moral education for delinquents.
3. Ethics of food technologists.
4. Problems of Hindus living in USA.
5. Collections of literature for social workers.
6. Experimental schools for non-literates.
7. Works on physical fitness for administrators.
8. Works on recreational arts for amateurs.
9. Works on animal husbandary for circus performers.
10. Collections of literature for philosophers.
11. Bibliographies of works by women authors.
12. Customs of Muslims.

Solutions

1. 635.024042
2. 370.114088364
3. 174.9664
4. 305.6945073
5. 808.89923362
6. 371.04088633
7. 613.70243532
8. 700.240909
9. 636.0247913
10. 808.899211
11. 013.042
12. 390.42971

X

SPECIAL TABLES (ADD TABLES)

The special tables are specifically being provided in DDC for specific subjects and are termed as Add Tables. These are being explained as 'Sets of tabulated numbers found in add notes under specific numbers throughout the Schedules and occasionally in Tables 1 to 7. These tabulated numbers are called add tables'.[1]

In recent times the provision for special tables has become a significant features of DDC. From Edition 18 onwards the scheme is gradually shedding off the image of enumerative scheme and stepping towards a more facted scheme. The addition of 7 auxiliary tables - out of which 4 tables may be used quite freely, the provision of special tables (add tables) and the increasing use of add-device, have made possible to provide co-extensive class numbers at least to macro-literature and thereby facilitating better service to readers. The anxiety of DDC Editorial Policy Committee to make the scheme more and more faceted is clearly visible from the new additions and modifications made in Special Tables in Edition 20. Followings are few such examples:

1. Special tables have now been provided for Historical Periods and for specific continents, countries, localities; extraterrestrial worlds in Table 1;
2. The provision of special table under 292-299 Religions other than Christianity in Edition 20 has done away with repetitive instructions provided for Standard subdivisions and use of numbers from 291.1-291.9 in Edition 19. Moreover this new modification in no way has affected the class numbers devised on the basis of Edition 19; e.g.:

   Title: Rites and ceremonies in Sikhism

Ed. 19	294.6	Sikhism
	.61-.69	Specific elements

[1]Glossary, DDC Vol. I Ed. 20 p57

Add to base number 294.6 the numbers following 291 in 291.1-291.9

[291.]38 Rites and ceremonies

C. No. 294.638

Ed. 20 In Edition 20 Sikhism is identified by † (dagger) directing to add as instructed under 291-299, through which the number for rites and ceremonies is used and the class number would be:

C. No. 294.638

3. Special table has also been provided in Edition 20 for 356-359 Specific kinds of military forces and warfare. This table has improved DDC in two ways: first, Edition 20 has done away with the repetitive enumeration of almost similar concepts under 356 to 359 and second the concepts required with a particular subject but not enumerated under it in Edition 19, have now uniform treatment as all the related concepts are enumerated in special table and may be used with all the identified numbers from 356-359,

Example:

Title: Uniforms of Commandos

Ed. 19 C. No. 356.15
(Number for uniforms not available)

Ed. 20 356.15 + 14 (Number for uniforms given under 356-359)

C. No. 356.1514

4. The special table for 368.1-368.8 Specific kinds of insurance has been improved upon. For example 0065 Insurance companies may be subdivided by adding Areas notation 4-9 from Table 2.

The special tables, therefore, have helped the DDC to avoid repetitive enumeration, when similar concepts are required by various specific subjects of a discipline. Thereby not only providing uniform and consistent sequence but also helping to follow Law of Parsimony and Canon of Mnemonics.

BROAD GUIDELINES FOR THE APPLICATION OF SPECIAL TABLE

The classifier should keep in view the following points when adding the numbers from special tables:

1. to verify the class numbers for which the special table is designed;
2. to read carefully the necessary instruction given for the use of the special table, e.g. the instruction that its numbers be added only to the numbers identified by * or † (asterisk or dagger).
3. the base number with which the number is to be added;
4. verify if under the notation of the Special Table to be used; any instruction to add further notations from Tables (Volume 1) or numbers from Schedules is given.

PRACTICE-STEPS TO BE USED

1. write base number of the specific subject;
2. add to it required notation from special table;
3. if any instruction under that notation is given, add further as per direction.

The special tables may be divided into two categories from the point of view of their use:

1. Special tables which may be used only when the number of the specific subject is identified by * (asterisk) or † (dagger).
2. Special tables the notation of which may be added directly to the number of specific subject.

1. USE OF SPECIAL TABLES THROUGH INDICATORS LIKE * (ASTERISK) OR † (DAGGER)

All such special tables which are to be used only through indicators, the classifier is specifically directed 'add to notation for each term identified by * or † :

Through this indicator three places are interlinked:

A Specific subject which is identified by * or † and to which notation of special table is to be added;

B *The footnote*: the * (asterisk) or † (dagger) directs the classifier to see the footnote instruction;

C And the place of special table as specified by the footnote instruction.

It is, therefore, imperative for the classifier that he moves in the right direction from specific subject to the special table. As he cannot add notation from special table unless the specific subject is identified.

Examples:

Title: Testing of glass

620.144 *Glass
Including fiber glass

0287 Testing (as under 620.12-620.19)

C. No. 620.1440287

Title: Teaching of social studies in elementary schools

372 Elementary education
.83 *Social studies
044 Teaching (as under 372.3-372.8)

C. No. 372.83044

2. SPECIAL TABLES–THE NOTATION OF WHICH MAY BE ADDED DIRECTLY

As a general rule this type of special tables have a prerequisite of Areas notation. In other words the numbers from this type of special table may be added only after Areas notation from Table 2; as the instruction to add numbers from special tables invariably reads as 'Add to base number...notation...from Table 2; then add further as follows'. In short, the numbers from this type of special tables may be added only after Areas notation and secondly, the numbers to which these are to be added are not identified by * or †. However, the special tables of the main class History is an exception to this, the numbers of which may be added directly or through identified numbers.

Examples:

Title: Management of Youth Hostels in India

647	Management of public households
647.943-.949	Treatment by specific continents...
	Add to base number 647.94 notation 3-9 from Table 2 then add further as follows:
07	Youth hostels
-54	India (Table 2)

C. No. 647.945407

Title: Role of communist parties in India

324.2	Political parties
342.24-.29	Treatment by specific continents
	Add to base number 324.2 notation 4-9 from Table 2; then add further as follows:
075	Communist parties
-54	India (Table 2)

C. No. 324.254075

Practical Problems

1. Development of urban lands.
2. Divinely inspired persons in Jain religion.
3. Theoretical chemistry of sulfur compounds.
4. Radiographic testing of titanium.
5. Elementary school curriculum for creative and manual arts.
6. Management of trailer camps in USA.
7. Legislative debates of India.
8. Social causes of suicide.
9. Complex compounds of thorium.
10. First aid in dental surgery.

Solutions

1. 333.7715
2. 294.463
3. 547.06044
4. 620.18932272
5. 372.5043
6. 647.947308
7. 328.5402
8. 362.281
9. 546.42225
10. 617.60262

XI

340 LAW

In Edition 20 there are minor modifications in the enumeration of subjects, use of notation, instructions and options in Main Class Law. But these modifications in no way need major changes in the libraries using Edition 19. Few such examples* are as follows:

1. **Ed. 19:** 340.1 / **Ed. 20:** 340 — Jurisprudence

2. The general guidelines and options are provided under:

Ed. 19:	340; 342-348 and .3-.9 Specific jurisdiction (more or less similar instructions and options are repeated.)
Ed. 20:	Only under 340 Law

3. Nomenclature of some of the classes have been changed without any change in their subdivisions:

Ed. 19:	340.5	Systems of Law
Ed. 20:	340.5	Legal Systems
Ed. 19:	340.52	Primitive Law
Ed. 20:	340.52	Law of traditional societies
Ed. 19:	342-348	Law of individual states and nations (Municipal Law) and laws, regulations, cases
Ed. 20:	342-348	Branches of law of specific jurisdictions and laws, regulations, cases

* Square brackets are used in all examples to indicate the numbers followings i.e. numbers not to be added.

Ed. 19:	343	Miscellaneous public law
Ed. 20:	343	Military, tax, trade, industrial law
Ed. 19:	344	Special law
Ed. 20:	344	Social, labour, welfare, health, safety, education, cultural law

PRACTICAL APPLICATION

The classifier is required to know the following for the proper and systematic handling of Main Class 340 Law.

1. Kinds of treaties under 341.026;
2. Procedure for classifying works on branches of law of specific jurisdictions and laws, regulations, cases.
3. The extended standard subdivisions - 026; enumerated in the main class itself; and
4. The Options

(1) 341 INTERNATIONAL LAW

The class number 341 and its subdivisions are used to enumerate various divisions of International Law, such as sources of International Law, relations between states, their conflicts and disputes as well as international treaties and cases.

341.026 TREATIES AND CASES:

The Standard subdivision notation -026 Law is being used in 341 International Law for subdividing different kinds of treaties and cases, e.g.:

341.026	Treaties and cases
341.0261-341.0266	Texts of treaties
341.0267	Codifications
341.0268	Cases

However, the classifier should note that 341.026 is to be used only for texts of treaties and judicial decisions and commentaries. Class comprehensive works on treaties in 341.37 and treaties as a source of law is to be classed in 341.1

The class numbers for series of treaties compiled by international organisations are enumerated from 341.0261–341.0263, e.g.:

341.0262 United Nations series of treaties

Add device is also used to individualise these treaties, e.g.:

Title: Series of treaties compiled by Asian regional associations and organisations

Base No.		**Add no. following 341.24**
341.0263	+	[341.24] 7

C. No. 341.02637

Similarly the kinds of treaties, collections and individual treaties are to be classed under 341.0265–341.0266

341.0266 BILATERAL TREATIES:

In case of bilateral treaties i.e. treaties between two nations, there are two directions for order of precedence of the country:

1. Give priority in notation to the country coming first in the sequence of the Areas notation.
2. (Option) Give priority in notation to the country requiring local emphasis.

PRACTICE-STEPS TO BE USED

(i) write base number 341.0266;

(ii) add to it the Areas notation for first nation from Table 2 as per directions given above;

(iii) to this number add 0;

(iv) then add notation for second nation from Table 2.

Examples:

Title: Treaties between France and United States of America

Base No.		**Areas notation coming first in sequence**		**Add**		**Areas notation second**
341.0266	+	-44	+	0	+	-73

C. No. 341.026644073

Title: Treaties between France and India.

Base No.		Areas notation local emphasis		Add		Areas notation
341.0266	+	-54	+	0	+	-44

C. No. 341.026654044

341.0268 CASES

Cases, decisions and reports on international matters are to be classed in 341.0268. Cases relating to two specific nations are to be classed in the following manner:

Title: Cases brought by Portugal against India in the International Court of Justice.

341.0268 Cases

Add to base number 341.0268 notation 4-9 from Table 2; then for cases brought by that nation against another nation add 0 and again add notation 3-9 from Table 2.

Base No.		Table 2 Cases brought by		Add		Table 2 against
341.0268	+	-469	+	0	+	-54

C. No. 341.0268469054

As a general rule the order of precedence as given in the instruction is to be followed. However, classifier has the option to give priority in notation to the nation requiring local emphasis. So Indian libraries may class the above case in:

C. No. 341.0268540469

342-348

(2) WORKS ON BRANCHES OF LAW OF SPECIFIC JURISDICTIONS AND LAWS, REGULATIONS, CASES

Uniform procedure is used to classify documents relating to divisions 342-348. Each division is subdivided in the following manner:

(2A) SUBDIVISIONS OF SPECIFIC BRANCH OF LAW

Base No.	+ Subdivisions	
342	+ 024	= Sources of constitutional law
348	+ 043	= State and provincial reports

(2Ai) This indicates that 0 is being utilised for enumerating the subdivisions of all the branches of law. In general readymade class numbers are available, e.g. :

Title: Environment Protection Law

C. No. 344.046

(2Aii) However, there are classes wherein the classifier is permitted to use add device to further sharpen or individualise the enumerated class numbers, e.g. :

Title: Law for working mothers

344.01 Labour

Add to base number 344.01 the numbers following 331 in 331.1–331.8

331.44 Working mothers

Base No.		Add numbers following 331
344.01	+	[331.]44

C. No. 344.0144

(2Aiii) Use of Standard subdivisions

With all such enumerated subdivisions the Standard subdivisions may be used directly as are used with other enumerated class numbers e.g.:

Title: Serial publications on Law of Evidence

345.06 Evidence

-05 Serial publication (SS Table 1)

C. No. 345.0605

(2B) BRANCHES OF LAW AND STANDARD SUBDIVISIONS

Base No.	+ Standard subdivisions		(Table 1)
342	+ -001	=	Theory of Constitutional Law
348	+ -001	=	Theory of the Laws of Statutes

As one zero is utilised for enumerating the subdivisions of the branches of law (as described above in A), it is necessary to use two zeros for Standard subdivisions. Therefore, under each number from 342-348 the instruction in this regard is given, e.g. :

Title: A study of the terminology used in Criminal Law

345 Criminal Law
Use 345.001-345.009 for Standard subdivision
-014 Language (Terminology) (SS Table 1)
-0014 as per instruction

C. No. 345.0014

(2C) LAW OF SPECIFIC JURISDICTIONS

Base No.		+Areas notation (Table 2)
342	+	.3 .9
348	+	.3-.9

The number .3-.9 is allotted in each branch of law from 342-348 to specific jurisdictions i.e. law of specific nations or states, etc. On the basis of the instruction provided under it the Areas notation from Table 2 may be added after the number for each branch of law, e.g.:

Title: Social law of Japan

344 Social law
.3-.9 Specific jurisdiction and areas
Add to base number 344 notation 3-9 from Table 2
-52 Japan (Table 2)

Base No.		Table 2
344	+	-52

C. No. 344.52

(2D) BRANCHES OF LAW, ITS SUBDIVISIONS AND SPECIFIC JURISDICTION

Title: Sources of Indian constitutional law

Base No.		Areas notation		subdivisions
342	+	-54	+	024

C. No. 342.54024

The procedure indicated above from A to C allows to use either subdivisions of the branches of law or specific jurisdictions. But if a document requires both the elements together to indicate the law of a nation and various related concepts, then the procedure given under .3-.9 specific jurisdictions is to be used. The procedure is as follows :

PRACTICE–STEPS TO BE USED

(i) write base number of the specific branch of law;

(ii) add to it required areas notation on the basis of the instruction given under .3-.9;

(iii) add to areas notation the number for required subdivision of the specific law on the basis of the instruction given under .3-.9 in each branch of law. Which States Add to base number...notation 3-9 from Table 2; then to the result add the numbers following.....

Titles: Balsara, SD. Criminal Procedure in Indian Legal System.

345 Criminal law

.3-.9 Specific jurisdictions and areas

Add to base number 345 notation 3-9 from Table 2 then to the result add the numbers following 345 in 345.001-345.087

-54	India (Table 2)
345.05	General Criminal procedure

Base No.		Table 2		Add numbers following 345
345	+	-54	+	[345.]05

C. No. 345.5405

(3) USE OF EXTENDED STANDARD SUBDIVISIONS

The notation -026 Law of Standard subdivisions (Table 1) has been extended in Main Class 340 Law to comply the specific needs of the discipline Law enumerated in 342-347. These extended Standard subdivisions may be added to terms identified by * (asterisk). In Edition 20 few minor modifications and changes have been made. These are :

(i) The add instructions in Edition 19 reads as 'Add to each subdivisions the following extended standard subdivisions'. In Edition 20 the necessary modification has been made as it now reads 'Add to each subdivisions identified by * the following extended notation'.

(ii) In Edition 20 the instruction that if required the Standard subdivisions (Table 1) may be added to 026 and its subdivisions is provided clearly under 026. In Edition 19 the rule is implicit in the general rule provided in the Editor's Introduction.

(iii) - 02633 Individual laws has been relocated to - 02632 together with collected laws.

Examples:

Title: Income tax laws and regulations

343.052	*Income tax (*add extended notation 026 as instructed under 342-347)
0263	Laws and regulations (as under 342-347)

C. No. 343.0520263

Title: Income tax law of India - laws and regulations

Base No.		Table 2		Subdivision of 343		Extended SS
343	+	-54	+	[343.]052	+	0263

C. No. 343.540520263

Title: Classification of Indian income tax law cases

Base No.		Table 2		Subdivisions of 343		Extended SS		SS (Table 1)
343	+	-54	+	[343.]052	+	-0264	+	012

C. No. 343.540520264012

OPTIONS

If this general sequence is not suitable to the needs of a particular library, the classifier is then allowed to use one of the following options to give local emphasis and shorter number to the law of preferred jurisdiction, area.

OPTION A

If it is desired to give local emphasis and a shorter number to a specific law of a specific jurisdiction or area, it is optional to use the class number of the specific law without geographical subdivision as the base number. This means;

(AI) BRANCH OF LAW AND ITS SUBDIVISIONS:

344	Social
344.04	Public health

If India is given preferred treatment as per Option A

344	Social law of India

When preferred treatment is given to specific jurisdiction the base number for specific branch of law would be used as the base number for preferred jurisdiction or area as follows :

(i) Specific branch of law, and

(ii) Preferred jurisdiction, area-India

344	Social law
344	Social law of India

and after this the number for enumerated subdivisions of the branch of law may be used, e.g.:

344.04	Public health law of India

(AII) SPECIFIC JURISDICTIONS, AREAS:

For classifying works on law relating to jurisdiction, area which is a subdivision of preferred jurisdiction or area the following procedure is to be used:

344 =	This includes social law + India
-54	India (Table 2) would not be used.
[-54]4	Rajasthan (Table 2) notation used for Rajasthan would only be used.

Examples:

Title: Public health law of Rajasthan

Base No.	**Table 2**	**Subdivision as of 344**
344	[-54]4	[344.]04

C. No. 344.404

The above procedure is also to be used for such subdivisions of a country which are indicated by irregular notation and do not look like subordinate divisions of that country, e.g.:

-624	Sudan	
-627	Darfar region of Sudan	Table 2
-628	Kordofan region of Sudan	

Public health law of these would be :

344	Social law of Sudan
344.7	Social law of Darfar region
344.704	Public health law of Darfar region
344.804	Public health law of Kordofan region.

If option A is used in a library then the number for specific branch of law cannot be used for law of other jurisdictions and areas. DDC therefore, instructs 'If option A is chosen then, class comprehensive works on the law of the preferred jurisdictions or area in 342; comparative law and the law of other jurisdictions and areas in 349'.

To comply with this the numbers following 34 are added to 349 e.g.:

349 + [34]5	
349.5	Criminal law
349.505	Criminal procedure
349.594	Criminal law of Australia
349.59405	Criminal procedure of Australia

This means that after 349 the number of specific branch is to be added after which same general rule is to be followed which is provided for works on law under 340.

OPTION B

ARRANGEMENT BY JURISDICTION OR AREA

Option B is for those libraries which opt for arrangement of documents by jurisdiction or area. These libraries have to follow the following procedure:

(i) write the base number 34 for law;

(ii) add to this areas notation from Table 2;

(iii) then add 0;

(iv) to the result add numbers for the branch of law i.e. numbers following 34 in 342-348;

(v) then add without 0 the subdivisions of the branch of law.

Examples:

Title: Criminal procedure Code of India.

34 + 54	Law of India
34 + 540	
34 + 540 + [34]5	Criminal law of India
34 + 540 + [34]5 + [0]5	Criminal Procedure Code of India
C. No. 345.4055	

If option B is followed, then class Comparative law and law without jurisdiction by adding to base number 342 the numbers following 34 in 342-348, but omitting the first zero after the decimal point, e.g., comparative criminals procedure 342.55 (not 342.505)

OPTION C

Class law of specific discipline or subject with the discipline or subject using notation 026 from Table 1, e.g.:

Library Legislation

C. No. 020.26

PRACTICAL PROBLEMS

1. Military Legal Procedures.
2. Indian criminal law cases.
3. Cases brought by United States against Iraq.
4. Powers and functions of British courts.
5. Roman-Dutch Law.
6. Descriptive research on Indian Public Works Law.
7. A digest of Income Tax Law cases.
8. Disarmament treaty between China and USA.
9. Treaty between the world health organisation and Spain on pollution control.
10. Rules and principles for legal practice.
11. Indian Copyright Law.
12. Debates on Indian Constitutional Law.
13. Series of treaties compiled by Atlantic Regional Associations and Organisations.
14. Law relating to trial of war criminals.
15. Privileges and immunities to witnesses in India.

Solutions

1. 343.0143
2. 345.540264

3. 341.0268730567
4. 347.41012
5. 340.56
6. 344.5406000723
7. 343.05202648
8. 341.026651073
9. 341.7623026
10. 347.0504
11. 346.540482
12. 342.540242
13. 341.2301
14. 341.69
15. 347.54066

XII

610 MEDICAL SCIENCES

In main class Medical Sciences the enumeration of subdivisions and use of numbers is uniform in both the Editions 19 and 20. However, the libraries which intend to change from Editions 19 and 20 should know that in Edition 20 there are some changes in regard to nomenclature, few modification and additions as well as shunting and shifting of some subjects, etc. A few such examples* are given below :

CHANGE IN NOMENCLATURE

612.3	Nutrition Ingestion, digestion...(Ed. 19)
	Digestion Class here nutrition (Ed. 20)
613	General and personal hygiene (Ed. 19)
	Promotion of health (Ed. 20)
614	Public health and related topics (Ed. 19)
	Forensic medicine, incidence of disease, public preventive medicine (Ed. 20)

Similar changes have been made in 614.4; 614.5; 616.86; 616.861; 616.97; 635; 637; 639; 672; 674 and 693. But these changes in the nomenclature create no problems as there is no change in the basic theme of the subjects, together with the subdivisions enumerated in both the editions.

CAUTION

(1) While classifying works on medical sciences, specially under 613-614, the classifier is required to read the thought content carefully, as the document may be related to 362 and not

* Square brackets are used in all examples to indicate the numbers followings i.e. numbers not to be added.

to 613 or 614. For example the numbers 613 and 614 deal with Promotion of health, Public health and related topics. Similarly, 362.1-362.4 deal with physical illness and disability. The confusion is more when the title of the document reads just Public health.

Neither 613 nor 614 include social provision of services to physically ill, but this is provided in 362.1. The direction how to differentiate between the two is clearly given in *DDC Manual*. It directs 'Use 613 and 614 and their subdivisions as long as the interest is scientific or technical. Once the emphasis shifts to social problems and services in connection with health problems, it should be classed in 362.1'.

For example: *Studies on alcoholism*. If it deals with addiction and personal aspects of prevention of alcoholism, it is to be classed in 613.81 but if it deals with alcoholism as a social problem i.e. remedial measures, services and forms of assistance, then it is to be classed in 362.2928. Similar problems may arise with documents on diseases as social problems or on medical aspects of diseases.

Note: If the classifier has any doubt between the two, then he is advised to prefer 360 and its subdivisions.[1]

(2) In Edition 20, there are some new interpolated numbers, some relocated and discontinued numbers. However, some of the discontinued numbers do create some doubt about the policy of DDC, as the subjects of these discontinued numbers have been shifted to broad numbers, directing the classifier to class such subjects in broad numbers. Few such cases are as follows:

	Edition 19	**Edition 20**
615.1901	Analysis	615.1901 Analysis
.19015	Chemical analysis	numbers discontinued;
.19018	Assay analysis	class in 615.1901
615.6	Methods of medication	615.6 Methods of
.61	Oral medication	medication numbers
.62	Rectal medication	discontinued;
.63	Parental medication	class in 615.6

[1]DDC Manual Vol. 4, Ed. 20 pp 897-898.

.64	Inhalatory medication
.66	Medication through...
.67	External medication

Those libraries which want to change to Edition 20, are required to give sufficient thought before using these broad numbers.

PRACTICAL APPLICATION

For practical classification, the Schedule for Medical Sciences may be categorised as follows :

(i) The enumerated numbers. In other words readymade class numbers.

(ii) Use of enumerated class numbers together with Special Tables.

(iii) Use of enumerated class numbers subdivided by Add Device.

(I) ENUMERATED CLASS NUMBERS

In so far as enumerated class numbers are concerned, these are to be used as are provided in the Schedule, e.g.:

Title: Epidemiology.

C. No. 614.4

Title: Bariatric surgery

C. No. 617.43

(II) SPECIAL TABLES

The main class 610 Medicine includes three Special Tables for:

616.1-616.9	Specific diseases
617	Surgery
618.1-618.9	Gynocology and obstetrics

Uniform treatment is given to these Special Tables both in

Edition 19 and 20. The notation of these Special Tables may be added only to class numbers for which these are designed and that too only to terms which are identified by *(asterisk)

PRACTICE-STEPS TO BE USED

(i) verify if the specific term with which the notation of Special Table is to be added is identified by *(asterisk); if yes

(ii) write the base number of the specific subject;

(iii) read the footnote instruction to know the place of Special Table designed for this specific subject;

(iv) add to required notation from the Special Table to base number of the specific subject;

(v) if under the notation of Special Table Add instruction is given, then add further as instructed.

SPECIAL TABLE FOR 616.1–616.9 SPECIFIC DISEASES:

...add to the notation for each term identified by *(asterisk) as 'follows'. The following few notations of this Table are:

001 Philosophy and theory

003-006 Standard subdivisions

07 Pathology

Add to 07 the numbers following 616.07 in 616.071-616.079

Examples:

Title: Theory and philosophy of diseases of endocrine system

616.4 Diseases of endocrine system

001 Philosophy and theory (Sp. Table)

C. No. 616.4001

Title: Radiological diagnosis of lung diseases.

616.24* Of lung

07 Pathology (Sp. Table)

[616.07]57 Radiological diagnosis (as per instruction under 07 pathology)

C. No. 616.240757

SPECIAL TABLE FOR 617 SURGERY

'add to notation for each term identified by *(asterisk) as follows': The following few notations of this Table are:

001-007	Standard subdivisions
01	Surgical complications and sequelae

Example:

Title: Surgical complications in brain surgery

617.481	*Brain
01	Surgical complications (Special Table)

C. No. 617.48101

SPECIAL TABLE FOR 618.1-618.8 GYNAECOLOGY AND OBSTETRICS

'add to the notation for each term identified by *(asterisk) as follows'. Following few notations of this Table are:

001-008	Standard subdivisions
061	Drug therapy
07	Pathology

Examples:

Title: Drug therapy used in the functional and systematic disorders in females

618.17	*Functional and systemic disorders
061	Drug therapy (Special Table)

C. No. 618.17061

EXCEPTIONS

There are some exceptions to the general rule that the notation of Special tables are to be added to the class numbers only for which this special Table is designed. For example the diseases enumerated from 616.992 to 616.99419 are identified by †(dagger) directing to use notation from the Special Table designed for 618.1-618.8 instead the notation of the Special Table for 616.1-616.9 specific diseases.

The classifier is, therefore, required to read the foothote directions carefully before adding notations from these Special Tables.

ADD DEVICE

Besides the provision of three Special Tables, main class Medicine has also used add device quite frequently to provide additional elements to the enumerated class numbers. For example 13 classes enumerated between 612.01448 to 612.0157, the add device is being used 5 times. Even for 9 classes from 615.2–615.329 for various drugs add device is used 5 times. The frequent use of add device is also found within classes from 616 to 618 besides the provision of three Special Tables for these classes.

Examples:

Title: Recreational therapy for mental disorders.

Base No.		**Add nos. following 615.851**
616.8916	+	[615.851]53

C. No. 616.891653

Title: Cancer of lymphatic glands

Base No.		**Add nos. following 611**
616.994	+	[611.]46

C. No. 616.99446

618.9 PEDIATRICS AND GERIATRICS

618.92 PEDIATRICS

The classifier has also to take all necessary precautions while classifying documents relating to children diseases. All those diseases which are most often treated in children but remain life time problems, for example mums, are to be classed in 616 and not in 618.92. Only those diseases the occurrences of which remain limited to childhood be classed in 618.92. Similar caution is required with regard to works on surgery. For example, surgical specialities applied to children is to be classed in 617; both medical and surgical aspects of dentistry for children in 617.6.[2]

Secondly it is only through add device that the notations of Special Tables may be used with 618.92.

PRACTICAL APPLICATION

Only few ready-made class numbers are enumerated in 618.92. The classifier is required to use Standard subdivisions or add device to provide additional elements to 618.92 in the following manner:

A. USE OF STANDARD SUBDIVISIONS

As one and two zeros have been utilised for enumerating general and special topics of pediatrics three zeros have been used for Standard subdivisions, e.g.:

Title: A list of pediatric publications

Base No.		SS	Use of zeros as per instruction
618.92	+	-016	-00016

C. No. 618.9200016

B. GENERAL TOPICS

Documents describing general topics on pediatrics are to be classified under 618.92001-618.92009. However, the classifier is instructed to add notation 01-09 from Special Table under 616.1-616.9 to base number 618.920.

Example:

Title: Nature and duties of child specialists

Base No.		Special Table 616.1-616.9
618.920	+	023

C. No. 618.920023

Title: Use of thermography in pediatrics

Base No.		Special Table		Add nos. following 616.07
618.920	+	07	+	[616.07]54

[2]For detailed information see DDC Manual, Vol. 4, Ed. 20.

C. No. 618.9200754

The classifier may also note that together with add instruction, the direction is also given that the pediatric preventive measures are to be classed in 613.0432 and pediatric therapeutics in 615.542.

C. REGIONAL MEDICINE

If the documents are related to the treatment of various parts of the body of a child, then these are to be classified under 618.920975 as the base number and adding to it numbers following 617.5 in 617.51–617.58.

Examples:

Title: Disorders in the throat of children

Base No.		**Nos. following 617.5**
618.920975	+	[617.5]31

C. No. 618.92097531

D. OPTHALMOLOGY, OTOLOGY, AUDIOLOGY

Documents dealing with disease pertaining to eye, ear and problems of hearing among children are to be classed in 618.92097 as the base number and adding to it the numbers following 617 in 617.7-617.8.

Examples:

Title: Colour blindness in children

Base No.		**Nos. following 617**
618.92097	+	[617.]759

C. No. 61892097759

E. SPECIFIC DISEASES OF FEMALE CHILDREN

To base number 618.920981 the numbers following 618.1 in 618.11-618.19 are to be added to individualise the gynec problems among female children.

Example:

Title: Diseases of ovaries in female children

Base No.		**Nos. following 618.1**
618.920981	+	[618.1]1

C. No. 618.9209811

F. SPECIFIC DISEASES IN CHILDREN

The class numbers enumerated from 616.1-616.9 are to be added to base number 618.92 to individualise the specific diseases in children.

Example:

Title: Common cold in children

Base No.		**Nos. following 616**
616.92	+	[616.]205

C. No. 618.92205

If necessary, the notation of Special Table under 616.1-616.9 may be added to the specific diseases in children in the same manner as with the diseases enumerated from 616.1-616.9.

Example:

Title: First aid in the functional disorders in children

616.342 *Functional disorders

As the term functional disorders is identified by *(asterisk) the notation of Special Table may be added to it. Therefore to the above class number for functional disorders in children, the notation of Special Table may be added in the following manner:

Base No.		**Nos. following 616**		**Special Table**
618.92	+	[616.]342	+	0252

C. No. 618.923420252

618.97 GERIATRICS

Works on diseases of persons in late adulthood are to be classified in 618.97. However, caution is required while classifying works related to other branches of medicine. For example, surgical specialities applied to persons in late adulthood is to be classed in 617; comprehensive works on geriatrics surgery in 617.97, dental surgery in 617.6050846, geriatrics preventive measures in 613.0438 and therapeutics in 615.547. Only diseases which are specifically related to old age are to be classed with base number 618.97 and adding to it all the numbers enumerated from 616 to 618 to individualise the specific diseases.

Examples:

Title: Diseases of joints in old age

Base No.		**Nos. following 61**
618.97	+	[61]6.72

C. No. 618.97672

USE OF THE NOTATION OF SPECIAL TABLES

The notation of three Special Tables which are provided for 616-618 may be added to 618.97 in two different ways.

1. Special Table for 616.1-616.9

The term geriatrics is identified by *(asterisk), which directs the classifier to act as per footnote instruction. The footnote instruction allows the use of the notation of Special Table provided for 616.1-616.9. It means these notations may be added directly to 618.97.

Example:

Title: How helpful are domestic medicines in curing diseases of old age

Base No.		**Special Table notation**
618.97	+	024

C. No. 618.97024

2. The notation of all the three Special Tables may also be used with the help of the add device provided to add to base number 618.97 the numbers following 61 in 616-618. It means if the terms added to base number 618.97 is identified by *(asterisk) the notation of Special Table may be added after the class number for that term in the following manner:

Base N.	Nos. following 61	Notation of Special Table	
618.97	+ [61]6.616 * Rental failure	+ 09	= 618.97661609
618.97	+ [61]7.48 * Nervous system	+ 0262	= 618.977480262
618.97	+ [61]8.142 * Infections	+ 09	= 618.97814209

This makes clear that the classifier may add notation of all the Special Tables as per direction of DDC given in 618.97 geriatrics.

Practical Problems

1. Neurosurgery.
2. How useful is streptomycin.
3. Biosynthesis of proteins.
4. Physical diagnosis of tumors in the digestive systems.
5. Prevention of malaria.
6. A study of anesthesiology.
7. Possibilities of curing epilepsy in childhood by drug treatment.
8. Control of diseases in underdeveloped countries.
9. Harmful effects of sedatives.
10. Abdominal disorders in children.
11. History of epidemics in Asia.
12. Research on the diseases of newborn infants.
13. Artificial limbs.
14. Drug therapy for communicable diseases.
15. Test-tube babies.

Solutions

1. 617.48
2. 615.32992
3. 612.01546
4. 616.99230754
5. 614.532
6. 617.96
7. 616.853061
8. 614.422724
9. 615.782
10. 618.9209758
11. 614.495
12. 618.9201072
13. 617.58
14. 616.90461
15. 618.178059

XIII

636 ANIMAL HUSBANDRY

In Edition 19 and 20 uniform treatment is given to the main class 636 Animal Husbandry. However, the following few minor changes have been introduced in Edition 20.

1. In Edition 20, the single level summary for specific animals is provided in the beginning immediately under the main class number. Whereas the place of summary for Generalities remains the same as that of Edition 19.
2. 636.08 The nomenclature of the term Generalities has been changed to Production and maintenance, animals for specific purposes, veterinary sciences.
3. 636.101-636.808 The nomenclature of the term General principle has also been changed to Ranches and farms, young production and maintenance of...for specific purposes, veterinary sciences in Edition 20.

PRACTICAL APPLICATION

The class numbers for production, maintenance and training of livestock and other domestic animals are enumerated in 636 from 636.01-636.08.

The method which is used in Zoological Sciences for specific animals and groups of animals is used in this main class also. That is under the class number of each species of animal the class numbers enumerated in the beginning of the main class i.e. from 636.01-636.08 are used through add device. Instead of providing a Special Table and a common instruction, it repeats the instruction under each class number for specific animal.

Secondly, the notations enumerated from 636.01-6.336.08 cannot be used with the specific breeds and kinds of animal wherein no add instruction is given. Therefore, a document related to training, care and maintenance of specific breeds or kinds of animal can not be assigned a coextensive class number. DDC could easily make it possible by using its 'asterisk device' and providing Special Table.

From the point of view of practical application the schedule for 636 Animal Husbandry may be divided in three parts:

1. Generalities/Production, maintenance, animal for specific purposes.
2. Specific animals.
3. Veterinary Sciences

1. GENERALITIES/PRODUCTION, MAINTENANCE, ANIMALS FOR SPECIFIC PURPOSES

636.01–636.08 have been used to enumerate readymade class numbers for production, maintenance, training, breeding of animals and different purposes for which the animals in general may be used e.g.:

636.083	Care and maintenance
636.0883	Food animals

2. SPECIFIC ANIMALS

From 636.1–636.9 class numbers for specific kinds of breeds of animals are enumerated. However, to provide them additional element the numbers from 636.01 to 636.08 may be added through add device. Even from the point of view of add device there are three categories:

2A. TO ADD NUMBERS TO ONE BASE NUMBER

For horse, dogs and cats there is one instruction and one base number provided under these animals to which all the numbers following 636.0 may be added; e.g.:

Title: **(i) Feed and nutrition for horses**
(ii) Care and maintenance of dogs
(iii) Cats as pets

	Base No.		Nos. following 636.0		C. No.
(i)	636.10	+	[636.0]85	=	636.1085
(ii)	636.70	+	[636.0]83	=	636.7083
(iii)	636.80	+	[636.0]887	=	636.80887

2B. TWO DIFFERENT BASE NUMBERS FOR ONE AND THE SAME ANIMAL

For cattle and sheep the numbers from 636.01-636.08 may be added with two different base numbers. One for Ranches, farms, production, maintenance and veterinary sciences, and another for Specific purposes. These are to be used in the following manner:

a. For Ranches, farms, production, etc...

With the base number provided in the add instruction numbers following 636.0 may be added as follows:

	Base No.		Nos. following 636.0		C. No.
(i)	636.20	+	[636.0]82	=	636.2082
(ii)	636.30	+	[636.0]83	=	636.3083

b. For Specific purpose

Second base number for above animals is given under the Specific purpose in the add instruction under it:

	Base No.		Nos. following 636.088		C. No.
(i)	636.21	+	[636.088]42	=	636.2142
(ii)	636.31	+	[636.088]3	=	636.313

The difference is quite clear. In the first base number, the numbers following 636.0 are to be added, while in second, numbers following 636.088 are to be added. Although in the first instruction the numbers from 636.01-636.08 are to be added, i.e. the numbers 636.088 are also included in it, but DDC specifically directs the classifier that for Specific purposes this base number is not to be used and it is therefore obligatory for the classifier to use second base number for Specific purposes.

2C. THREE DIFFERENT BASE NUMBERS FOR ONE AND THE SAME ANIMAL

The three different base numbers are provided for 636.39 goats, 636.4 swine and 636.5 chickens. To these base numbers the numbers following 636.0 are added in the following manner:

(i) For Ranches, farms, production

Base No.

636.390

636.40 To these base numbers, numbers following 636.0 are
636.50 added in the same manner as in 2B(a) e.g.

636.390 + [636.0]82 = 363.39082

636.40 + [636.0]83 = 363.4083

(ii) For Specific purposes

Base No.

636.391 To these base numbers, numbers
636.41 following 636.088 are added in the
636.51 same manner as in 2B(b) e.g.

636.41 + [636.088]42 = 636.4142

636.51 + [636.088]3 = 636.513

(iii) Specific breeds

For all kinds of animals and their different breeds readymade class numbers are enumerated. It is only for the specific breeds of goats, and European breeds of swine and chickens that add device is used to add numbers following 636.3 in 636.32-636.37.

636.392 - .398 Specific breeds of goats

Examples:

Title: African goats

Base No.		**Add nos. following 636.3**
636.39	+	[636.3]86

C. No. 636.3986

636.52 - .57 European breeds of chickens

Title: Spanish merino chickens

Base No.		**Add nos. following 636.3**
636.5	+	[636.3]66

C. No. 636.566

OTHER ANIMALS

For 636.6 Birds only enumerated numbers are to be used, whereas 636.9 other mammals are to be subdivided on the basis of 599 Mammalia (Mammals) in the following manner:

Title: Care and maintenance of camels

Base No.		**Add nos. following 599**
636.9	+	[599.]736

C. No. 636.9736

636.089 VETENARY SCIENCE VETERNARY MEDICINE

One of the unique example of 'Add device' used by DDC is in the Veterinary Sciences 636.089. Veterinary Sciences/Veterinary medicine is to be extended on the analogy of Medical Sciences 610. The whole schedule for Medicine may be transformed into the Schedule for Veterinary Sciences/Veterinary Medicine on the basis of add instruction provided under 636.089 which directs to add to base number 636.089 the numbers following 61 in 610-619. For example:

Base No.		**Nos. following 61**	**C. No.**	
636.089	+	[61]1	636.0891	Anatomy of animals
636.089	+	[61]2	636.0892	Physiology animals
636.089	+	[61]6	636.0896	Diseases of animals

This makes quite clear that the numbers from the whole of the Schedule for Medicine together with its Special Tables may be added to Animal Husbandry through 636.089 Veterinary Sciences.

Examples:

Title: Diagnosis and prognosis of animal diseases

Base No.		**Nos. following 61**	**C. No.**
636.089	+	[61]6.075	636.0896075

Title: Orthopedic surgery of animals

Base No.		Nos. following 61	C. No.
636.089	+	[61]7.3	636.08973

SPECIFIC ANIMALS

The numbers of the Schedule for Medicine may also be added to the class numbers enumerated for specific animals from 636.1-636.8. But it is only through 636.089 that the numbers from the Schedule for Medicine may be added in the following manner:

Examples:

Title: Digestive tract organs of horses

Base No.		Nos. following 636.0		Nos. following 61
636.10	+	[636.0]89	+	[61]1.3

C. No. 636.108913

Title: Skin ulcerations in cats

Base No.		Nos. following 636.0		Nos. following 61
636.80	+	[636.0]89	+	[61]6.545

C. No. 636.80896545

NOTATIONS OF THREE SPECIAL TABLES:

Through 636.089 the class numbers of all the terms enumerated in 610 may be added. Similarly the notations of three Special Tables may be added through 61 to 636.089 in the following manner:

Examples:

Title: Drug therapy used for functional disorders in dogs.

616.332 *Functional disorders. (As it is identified by * (asterisk) so notation of Special Table may be added to it).

Base No.		Nos. following 636.0		Nos. following 61		Special Table for 616
636.70	+	[636.0]89	+	[61]6.332	+	061

C. No. 636.70896332061

Title: Drug therapy for blast injuries in animals

617.19 *Blast injuries

Base No.		Nos. following 61		Special Table for 617
636.089	+	[61]7.19	+	061

C. No. 636.089719061

Practical Problems

1. Ranches of horses.
2. Dry fodder for chickens.
3. Rabbit as domestic animal.
4. Dogs used for experimental research.
5. British breeds of swine.
6. Care of ornamental birds.
7. Training of Tibetan terrier.
8. An index of cattles of British breeds.
9. Training dogs for hunting.
10. Care and maintenance of cats.
11. Ownership marks on sheep.
12. Production of goats for wool.
13. Drug therapy used for the treatment of functional disorders in animals.
14. Regional surgery for animals.
15. Biopsis in Cattle.

Solutions

1. 636.101
2. 636.508554
3. 636.9322
4. 636.700724
5. 636.42
6. 636.68
7. 636.72

8. 636.22016
9. 636.70886
10. 636.8083
11. 636.30812
12. 636.39145
13. 636.0896332061
14. 636.08975
15. 636.208960758

XIV

900 GEOGRAPHY, HISTORY AND AUXILIARY DISCIPLINES

In the main class 900 Geography, History and Auxiliary Disciplines there are no major changes in Edition 20. The enumeration of subjects and their class numbers are similar in Editions 19 and 20. Whatever minor modifications and changes that have been introduced in Edition 20, in no way hinders a library from changing from Edition 19 to 20.

The heading of the main class itself indicates a minor modification, as the heading 'General geography and history and their auxiliaries' of Edition 19 reads as 'Geography, history and auxiliary disciplines' in Edition 20.

The main class 900 deals with following main subjects:

1. General geography
2. History
31. General biography
32. Genealogy, names, insignia

However subjects like social situations and conditions, general political history, military, diplomatic, political, economic, social welfare aspects of specific wars may also be classed in Main class 900.

PRACTICAL APPLICATION

From the point of view of practical application of the main class 900, it may be subdivided in the following manner:

1. 900.1-900.9 Standard subdivisions of geography and history
2. 910-919 Geography and travel
3. 920-929 Biography, Genealogy, insignia
4. 901.909; 939-990 History

(1) 900.1-900.9 STANDARD SUBDIVISIONS OF GEOGRAPHY AND HISTORY

As per enumeration in the Schedule two zeros are to be used for Standard subdivisions of geography and history when both the subjects are described together in the document, e.g.:

Title: Serial publications of history and geography

C. No. 900.5

Title: Organisations of geography and history

C. No. 900.6

(2) 910-919 GEOGRAPHY AND TRAVEL

The main divisions which the class number from 910-919 include are:

(21) 910.02 PHYSICAL GEOGRAPHY

Documents dealing with the areas, regions and places in general only are to be classed in 910.02. However, documents dealing with physical geography of specific continents, countries are to be classed in 939-990 using notation 02 from Special Table.

Example:

Title: Physical geography of coastal regions

910.02 + 146 = C. No. 910.02146

However, the classifier may note that there is difference in the base number and language of the add instruction in Editions 19 and 20, which in no way affects the class number so devised.

910.02 The earth (Physical geography)

Edition 19 : Add to Areas notation 1 from Table 2 to base number 910.02

Edition 20 : Add to base number 910.021 the numbers following 1 in notation 11.18 from Table 2

Example:

Title: Physical geography of rural regions

	Base No.	Table 2
Ed. 19	910.02	-1734
Ed. 20	910.021	[-1]734*

C. No. 910.021734

(22) 910.1 TOPICAL GEOGRAPHY

In DDC two different class numbers are assigned to the various kinds of geography related to specific subjects:

(A) Under 910.1
(B) Under related discipline or subject

910.1 Topical Geography:

(A) With the help of the instruction provided under 910.1 class numbers for various kinds of geography related to specific subjects may be devised.

Examples:

Title: Economic geography of India.

910.1	Topical geography Add 001-899 to base number 910.1, then add 0 and to the result add notation 1-9 from Table 2
330	Economics
-54	India (Table 2)

Base No.		Add number from 001-899		Add zero		Add Areas notation
910.1	+	33[0]	+	0	+	-54

C. No. 910.133054

(B) However, according to the DDC direction the use of this number is optional and the preference should be given to the specific subject, e.g.:

330.9 Economic geography

* Square brackets are used in all examples to indicate the numbers following i. e. numbers which are not to be added

355.47	Military geography
525	Astronomical geography
526	Mathematical geography

(23) 910.3 DICTIONARIES, GAZETTERS

General geographical dictionaries, concordances, gazetteers and works on place names systematically arranged for ready reference are to be classed in 910.3 both in Editions 19 and 20.

Examples:

Title: Webster's geographical dictionary, rev. ed. 1972

C. No. 910.3

Title: Statesman's yearbook World Gazetteer, edited by John Paxton, London 1988

C. No. 910.3

TRAVEL

The numbers relating to travel may be grouped into :-

(1) 910 Travel general treatment

(2) 913-919 Travel in specific continents, countries...

(1) 910 Travel general treatment

DDC has enumerated more or less ready made class number under 910, e.g.:

910.202	World travel guide
910.4	Accounts of travel
910.41	Trips around the world

However, there is one change in Edition 20 as 910.09 has been relocated to 910.91. Hence the documents dealing with Geography of and travel in areas, regions places in general would be classed in 910.09 in Edition 19 and in 910.91 in Edition 20.

Discovery and Exploration:

910.93-.99	By specific countries
913-919	In specific continents, countries
	(Treatment in Editions 19 and 20 is similar)

Note: (i) that all the documents describing discoveries and exploration by one specific country in general are to be classed in 910.9 e.g.:

Title: Discoveries by Portugese

Base No.		**Areas number for country responsible Table 2**
910.9	+	-469

C. No. 910.9469

Title: Exploration by United States

Base No.	**Table 2**
910.9	-73

C. No. 910.973

(ii) that those documents which describe excursions into previously unknown or little known areas are to be classed in 913–919 using 04 from special table under 913-919, e.g.:

Title: Exploration by India of Antarctica

Base No.		**Areas**		**Special Table**
91	+	-989	+	04

C. No. 919.8904

Title: Exploration by United States of Antarctica in 20th Century

Base No.		**Table 2**		**Special Table**		**Nos. following 973**
91	+	-989	+	04	+	[973.]9

C. No. 919.89049

(iii) that if the initial exploration of a place forms an important part of the early history of a country, then it is to be classed in 930-990, e.g.:

Title: French explorations in North America

C. No. 970.018

Title: Spanish discovery and exploration in Panama, 1501-1515

C. No. 972.8012

911 HISTORICAL GEOGRAPHY

Documents describing growth and changes in political divisions of specific countries, localities are to be classed in 911. This class number is also to be used for classifying historical atlases and maps.

Title: New political divisions of former USSR

Base No.		Table 2
911	+	-47

C. No. 911.47

Title: Historical maps of India

Base No.		Table 2
911	+	-54

C. No. 911.54

912 GRAPHIC REPRESENTATION OF SURFACE OF EARTH

The class number 912 includes graphic representation of surface of earth and extraterrestrial world in the form of maps, atlases, charts and plans.

Difference in Editions 19 and 20

Edition 19 has provisions for: 912.1001–912.1899 Maps, atlases, etc., of specific subject

Example :

Title: Maps locating monastic schools of Buddhism

Base No.		Add 001-899
912.1	+	377.3

C. No. 912.13773

This provision has been *discontinued* in Edition 20. The classifier is now directed to class subject maps, atlases with the specific subject itself using Standard subdivision notation -0223 from Table 1. In Edition 20, the Standard subdivisions - 0223 used for plans, diagrams is also used for maps and related forms.

MAPS RELATING TO SPECIFIC AREAS

There is no change in Edition 20 in so far as instruction to add notation from Table 2 for maps, atlases relating to specific country is concerned. However, there are two different instructions for classifying maps relating to areas, regions, places in general and specific continents, countries, etc. e.g.:

(A) 912.1 Maps of Areas, regions, places in general

Title: Maps of Arabian sea

Base No.		**Nos. following -1**
912.19	+	[-1]6537

C. No. 912.196537

Title: Maps locating Arab predominated regions

Base No.		**Nos. following -1**		**Table 5**
912.19	+	[-1]74	+	-927

C. No. 912.1974927

(B) 912.3-.9 Maps of specific continents, countries...

Title: Bihar in maps

Base No.		**Areas Table 2**
912	+	-5412

C. No. 912.5412

913-919

GEOGRAPHY OF AND TRAVEL IN ANCIENT WORLD AND SPECIFIC CONTINENTS, COUNTRIES LOCALITIES IN MODERN WORLDS; EXTRATERRESTRIAL WORLDS

DIFFERENCE IN EDITIONS 19 AND 20

1. In so far as the geography of and travel in ancient, modern

and extraterrestrial worlds is concerned, there is one improvement in Edition 20, which in no way affects the libraries using Edition 19. In Edition 19 the class numbers 913 the ancient world and 914-919 the modern worlds are treated separately both in enumeration and provision of Special Tables. Whereas in Edition 20 there is only one single Special Table for 913-919, in which the notation of both the Special Tables of Edition 19 have been enumerated. However, the class number so devised will be the same in both the Editions 19 and 20.

2. Secondly, the special table of Edition 19 only indicates through enumeration to use 001-009 for Standard subdivisions, whereas in Edition 20 these are further subdivided and specific directions are also provided under them, e.g.:

0014 Language (Terminology) communication

Class here discursive works on place names and there origin, history and meaning.

002 Miscellany

0022 Illustrations, models, miniatures

00222 Pictures and related illustrations,

Example: aerial photographs

Similar useful directions are available under other Standard subdivisions also, which the libraries using Edition 19 may also utilise.

Examples:

Title: Aerial photographs of some Interior regions of India

Base No.		Areas Table 2		Special Table use 001-008 for SS
91	+	-54	+	-00222

C. No. 915.400222

Title: City directories and telephone books of Rajasthan

Base No.		Areas Table 2		Special Table use 001-008 for SS
91	+	-544	+	-0025

C. No. 915.440025

Title: Gazetteer of India. 4 Vols.

Base No.		**Areas Table 2**		**Special Table use 001-008 for SS**
91	+	-54	+	-003

C. No. 915.4003

USE OF OTHER NUMBERS OF THE SPECIAL TABLE 01-09

The numbers 01-09 are used for such subjects as:

- 01 Prehistoric geography
- 02 Physical geography
- 04 Travel
- 09 Areas, regions, places in general.

Under these numbers also better directions and explanations are available in Edition 20. However, there is no basic difference in the use of these numbers between the two editions e.g.

913-914 Geography of and travel in...

Add to base number 91 notation 3-9 from Table 2, then add further as follows:

01 Prehistoric geography

Title: Prehistoric geography of china

-31 Ancient China

Base No.		**Table 2**		**Special Table**
91	+	-31	+	01

C. No. 913.101

02 The earth (Physical geography)

Title: Physical geography of Rajasthan

-544 Rajasthan

Base No.		Table 2		Special Table
91	+	-544	+	02

C. No. 915.4402

04 Travel

Title: Narrative of a journey through upper provinces of India from 1824-1828 in 3 Vols.

04 Travel

041-049 Historical periods

Add to 04 the historical period numbers following 0 that appear in subdivisions of 930-990 e.g. :

954.0313 1807-1828

Base No.		Areas Table 2		Special Table number		No. following 0 in 939-990
91	+	-54	+	04	+	[954.0]313

C. No. 915.404313

09 Areas, regions, places in general

Add to 09 the numbers following -1 in notation 11-18 from Table 2.

Title: Geography of rural regions of India

-1734 Rural regions (Table 2)

Base No.		Table 2		Special Table		Table 2 nos. following -1
91	+	-54	+	09	+	[-1]734

C. No. 915.409734

BIOGRAPHY, GENEALOGY, INSIGNIA

Class here autobiographies, diaries, reminiscences, correspondence.

920 Biography is divided into two main divisions:

(1) General collections of biography
(2) Individual or collective biography of persons associated with specific discipline or subject

(1) *GENERAL COLLECTION OF BIOGRAPHY:*

This division may further be divided into four subdivisions:

(a) General collections of biography by period;
(b) General collections of biography by areas, regions, places;
(c) General collections of biography by racial, ethnic, national groups;
(d) General collections of biography not limited by period, place, group and not associated with specific subject.

(1A). GENERAL COLLECTIONS OF BIOGRAPHY BY PERIOD

A collection of biographies of persons who are associated with various disciplines or subjects or belonging to different areas, but are of a common period. Such a collection is to be classified under 920.00901–.00905 Historical periods.

PRACTICAL-STEPS TO BE USED

(1) write base number 920.0090;
(2) add numbers following 090 in "Standard Subdivisions" notation 0901-0905 from Table 1.

Examples:

Title : Current Biography Monthly, 1940, Ny, H.W. Wilson (Contains articles on important contemporary personalities in all fields)

Base No.		**Add numbers following -090 from Table 1**
920.0090	+	[-090]44

C. No. 920.009044

Title: Who's who, an annual biographical dictionary, 1849, London

Base No.		Add numbers following -090 from Table 1
920.0090	+	[-090]34

C. No. 920.009034

(1B) GENERAL COLLECTIONS OF BIOGRAPHY OF AREAS, REGIONS

A general collection of biography not associated with a specific discipline or subject or time or national, racial, ethnic group, but relating to regions, places in general or to specific continents, countries, localities, then such a biography is to be classified on the basis of the Areas notation 1-9 from Table 2.

In DDC biography by Areas has two different base number:

Biography by Areas

	Base number 920.0091		Base number 920.0
(1Ba)	Biography by areas, regions, places in general	(1Bb)	Biography by specific continents, countries, localities

(1Ba) 920.0091 Areas, Regions, Places in General

A general biography of persons not associated to a specific continent, country or locality but associated to general physiographic regions or socioeconomic regions or other kinds of terrestrial regions is to be classified under 920.009.

Difference in Editions 19 and 20

In Edition 20 the Add instruction directs to 'Add to base number 920.0091 the numbers following -1 in notation 11-19 from Table 2'. *This means*

(a) The difference in base number;

Ed. 19	920.009
Ed. 20	920.0091

(b) Difference in the instruction for Add Areas notation from Table 2.

Ed. 19	Add Areas notation -1 from Table 2

Ed. 20	Add the numbers following -1, e.g.:			
-1811	Eastern Hemisphere			
	Base No.		Areas Table 2	
Ed. 19	920.009	+	1811	= C. No. 920.0091811
Ed. 20	920.0091	+	[1]811	= C. No. 920.0091811

This makes clear that the difference in Add instruction in Editions 19 and 20 has not made any change in the class number so devised.

Examples:

Title: Who is who in Afro-Asian bloc

	Base No.		Areas Table 2	
Ed. 19	920.009	+	- 17165	= C. No. 920.00917165
Ed. 20	920.0091	+	[-1]7165	= C. No. 920.00917165

Title: Biographies of eminent living personalities in underdeveloped countries of the world

	Base No.		Areas Table	
Ed. 19	920.009	+	-1724	= C. No. 920.0091724
Ed. 20	920.0091	+	[-1]724	= C. No. 920.0091724

(1Bb) 920.03-.09 General Collections of Biography By Continents, Countries, Localities

(Treatment in Editions 19 and 20 is similar)

A general collection of biography of persons not associated with one specific subject but belong to specific continents, countries or localities, such collections of biography is to be classified under 920.03-.09

Examples:

Title: Dictionary of national biography edited by S P Sen, Calcutta, 4 Vols

Base No.		Areas Table 2
920.0	+	-54

C. No. 920.054

Title: **Dictionary of national biography, edited by Leslie Stephen and sidney Lee, 21 Vols (cover 32,000 biographical sketches of eminent deceased persons of Great Britain)**

Base No.		**Areas Table 2**
920.0	+	-41

C. No. 920.041

(1 C) GENERAL COLLECTIONS OF BIOGRAPHY BY RACIAL, ETHNIC, NATIONAL GROUPS

General collections of biography of one racial, ethnic or national group, although not residing in one specific continent, country or locality or not associated with one specific discipline or subject is to be classified under 920.0092 and adding to it, notation from Table 5.

Examples:

Title: A collective biography of Indians

Base No.		**Table 5**
920.0092	+	-91411

C. No. 920.009291411

Title: **A general collections of biography of Spanish Americans**

Base No.		**Table 5**
920.0092	+	-68

C. No. 920.009268

(1D) GENERAL COLLECTIONS OF BIOGRAPHY NOT LIMITED BY PERIOD, PLACE, GROUP AND NOT ASSOCIATED WITH SPECIFIC SUBJECTS

A general collection of biography which may not be limited to one of the prescribed criteria for classifying collections of biography i.e. the historical periods, areas, racial, ethnic, national groups of persons associated with specific subject is to be classed in 920.02. In other words a collection of biography may cover all or more than one of the above criteria, is to be treated as a purely general collection of biography.

Examples:

Title: Chambers biographical dictionary: The Great of all national and of all times, rev. edition. N.Y.

C. No. 920.02

Title: Webster's biographical dictionary; rev ed. 1972

C. No. 920.02

(2) *920.1-928.9 INDIVIDUAL OR COLLECTIVE BIOGRAPHY OR PERSONS ASSOCIATED WITH SPECIFIC DISCIPLINE OR SUBJECT.*

OPTIONS

There are two options to classify biography of specific classes of persons;

(A) The numbers from 920.1-928.9 biography of specific classes of persons are optional numbers. DDC directs the classifier to prefer the number for specific subject or discipline with which the person is associated using the Standard subdivision notation -092 from Table.

(B) An individual biography may also be classed in 92 or B and a collected biography in 92 or 920 undivided.

Difference in Editions 19 and 20

There is one improvement in Edition 20. In the beginning that is under 920.1-928.9, one general Add instruction is provided which directs the classifier to 'Add to notation for each term identified by †(dagger) notation 3-9 from Table 2'. In Edition 19 this instruction has been repeated about 25 times under different class numbers from 920.1-928.9. Just one instruction in the beginning has saved the unnecessary repetition in Edition 20.

PRACTICAL APPLICATION

(i) Biography of persons associated with specific subject or discipline is to be classed in the specific subject or discipline; it is option to class in 920.1-928.9 e.g.:

Title: Biography of Dr. S.R. Ranganathan

020.924 (Ed. 19) or 920.2
020.92 (Ed. 20)

(ii) Class numbers enumerated under 920.1-928.9 are devised on the basis of specific discipline or subject, i.e., by adding the class number for specific discipline or subject to 92, e.g.:

020	Library and Information Science
92 + 02 = 920.2	*Biography of librarians and book collectors*

(iii) The class number under which instruction to Add Areas or languages notation or numbers from the Schedules is given may be subdivided as per instruction, e.g.:

(iiia) Add Areas notation 3-9 from Table 2

Title: Biography of Prof. VKRV Rao a renowned economist of India

Base No.		**Areas Table 2**
923.3	+	-54

C. No. 923.354 or 330.092 (using SS notation -092)

(iiib) Add notation from Table 6

Title: Collections of biography of fiction writers in Hindi language

Base No.		**Table 6**
928	+	-91431

C. No. 928.91431

(iiic) Add from Schedules 001-999

Title: Who's who in magic and witchcraft from past to present

Base No.		**Add from 001-999**
920.9	+	133.43

C. No. 920.913343 or 133.43092 (using SS notation -092)

Title: Biography of Sunil Gawaskar - Little Master !

Base No.		Add numbers following 7
927	+	[7] 96.358

C. No. 927.96358 or 796.358092 (using SS notation -092)

BIOGRAPHIES COVERING MAIN CLASS 900 GEOGRAPHY AND HISTORY

1. Class a general collections of biography of historians and historiographer in 907.202
2. Class the biography of individual historian and historiographer who specialises in World history in 907.202 and *not* in 909.2.*
3. Biography of individual historians and historiographer who specialise in specific area is to be classed in the specific area in which he specialises using notation 007202 from Special Table for 930-990 e.g.:

   Title: Biography of an Indian historian who specialises in British history.

Base No.		Notation from Special Table under 939-999
941	+	007202

   C. No. 941.007202

4. However, if the individual historian or historiographer specialises in a specific historical period, then in place of 007202 the SS notation 092 from Table 1 is to be added after historical period 01-09 enumerated for specific continent, country under 939-990, e.g.:

   Title: Biography of an Indian Historian who specialises in Victorian period 1837-1901.

941	History of Great Britain
941.081	Victoria 1837-1901

*See Manual page 416 (Ed. 19) and page 913 (Ed. 20)

-092 Biography (SS Table 1)

C. No. 941.0810924 (Ed. 19)
C. No. 941.081092 (Ed. 20)

5. For biographies of discoverers, explorers and travelers SS notation -092 is to be added after 04 Travel of Special Table under 913-919. e.g.:

Title: General collections of biography of Indian travellers

Base No.		Table 2		Special Table		Table 1
91	+	-54	+	-04	+	-0922

C. No. 915.4040922

Title: Biography of an Indian traveller

Base No.		Table 2		Special Table 913 - 919	Table 1
91	+	-54	+	-04	-0924 (Ed. 19) -092 (Ed. 20)

C. No. 915.4040924 (Ed. 19)
C. No. 915.404092 (Ed. 20)

In Edition 20 the the notation - 0924 for Individual Biography has been discontinued.

However, biography of general geographer is to be classed in the base number for the area without further subdivision. It means the notation -92 would not be added to such a Biography. For first person accounts of travel use historical periods as directed under 04 in Special Table but do not add 092 from Table 1. The area covered by the travelers should be seen in the broader perspective, for example travel from kashmir to Kanyakumari should be classified under - 54 India.

929 GENEALOGY, NAMES, INSIGNIA

Genealogy means the history of the descents of families, the pedigree of a particular person or family, whereas insignia is sign or mark for identifying the official position, honour, status of a country, organisation, association, or individual.

929.1 GENEALOGY

This is the comprehensive number for works providing information about genealogy. This number is also used for techniques of compiling family history and how to use genealogical sources etc.

929.2 FAMILY HISTORIES

The classifier has the option to arrange family histories alphabetically by names. However, while classifying documents relating to family history the following points are to be kept in view:

(1) If the document describing family histories is emphasising more on the contributions of the members of the family to a specific occupation, then class it with the specific occupation, e.g.:

Title: The Tatas family of industrialists.

C. No. 338.0922

(2) If it is more a biographical description of one of the prominent persons of the family, then it is to be assigned the class number of biography of that person, e.g.:

Title: Family history and life of Indira Gandhi

C. No. 954.9220924 (Ed. 19)

C. No. 954.922092 (Ed. 20)

(3) The area number for family history should not be too specific. It is better to use the country number where the family lives rather than the state or smaller area number, e.g.:

Title: Life and history of Nehru family

C. No. 929.220954

(4) Class the family history with the country in which the family presently live, not with the country from which the family's ancestors came.

(5) If the document relating family histories provide historical information about the area in which the family live, then class such a document with the history of the area.

Example:

Title: History of Prominent families in Bombay city

C. No. 954.792

(6) History of a royal family is to be classed in 929.7 and not in 929.2

929.3 GENEALOGICAL SOURCES

All such records which are compiled for genealogical purposes are to be classed in 929.3. Such sources may be wills, tax lists, court records or census records published by a genealogical agency or by an individual person. Sources published by an agency or by the government should be classified in the subject, e.g.:

Title: Census records of India

C. No. 319.54

The class number 929.3 may further be subdivided by using Areas and historical periods, e.g.:

Title: Genealogical sources from 1920-1929

C. No. 929.309042

Title: Genealogical sources from Kashmir

Base No.		**Table 2**
929.3	+	-546

C. No. 929.3546

929.5-929.7 DIFFERENCE IN EDITIONS 19 AND 20

There are few following modifications in nomenclature, etc. in Edition 20. 929.5 assigned to Epitaphs in Edition 19 has been assigned to cemetery records in Edition 20 and epitaphs being cited as example under 929.5

929.7	Royal houses...
.7999	assigned in Edition 19 to countries outside Europe has been relocated to 929.709 Historical and geographical treatment in Edition 20.

929.8	Orders, decorations, autographs (in Edition 19)
.8	Awards, orders, decorations, armorial bearings, autographs (in Edition 20).
929.81	Orders and decorations (in Edition 19)
.81	Awards, orders, decoration (in Edition 20)

In Edition 20 add Areas instruction is also provided under 929.81, which is not available in Edition 19.

However, awards, orders, decorations associated with specific subjects are to be classed with the subject itself using notation -079 from Table 1.

GENERAL HISTORY

The numbers allotted to the discipline history may be divided in the following manner:

(1) 901-908 Standard subdivisions of history

(2) 909 World history

(3) 930-990 History of specific continents, countries, localities; of extraterrestrial worlds

(1) 901-908 STANDARD SUBDIVISIONS OF HISTORY

With the ready made Standard subdivision numbers, enumerated in the Schedule, the subdivisions enumerated in Table 1 may be added, e.g.:

Title: Chronological outlines of general history

C. No. 902.02

Title: An index to general history

C. No. 901.6

(2) 909 WORLD HISTORY

(This also includes civilization and events not limited geographically)

909 World history has the following main divisions:

(2A) 909.04 *History with respect to racial, ethnic, national groups*

(2B) 909.07-909.08 *General historical periods*

909.1-909.8 *Specific historical periods*

(2C) 909.09 *History with respect to Areas, regions, places in general.*

(2A) 909.04 RACIAL, ETHNIC, NATIONAL GROUPS

To individualise the world history of specific racial, ethnic, national groups classifier is directed to add notation from Table 5. This instruction is provided under 909.4 which is to be applied in the following manner:

(i) write base number 909.04;

(ii) to this add from Table 5 the required notation;

(iii) if historical period is also required then add 0 after the notation of Table 5;

(iv) then add numbers following 909 in 909.1-909.8

Example:

Title: World history of Indians

Base No.		**Table 5**
909.04	+	-91411

C. No. 909.0491411

Title: World history of Indians upto 19th Century

Base No.		**Table 5**		**Add**		**Nos. following 909**
909.04	+	-91411	+	0	+	[909.]81

C. No. 909.0491411081

OPTION

909.04 may also be used for general history of racial, ethnic, national groups.

As a general rule the documents relating to the general history of racial, ethnic, national groups are to be classed under specific continents, countries, localities 930-990 using subdivisions 004 of special table. However, the classifier has been given the option that he may classify general history of racial, ethnic, national groups in 909.04

IF OPTION IS USED

If this option is used then the classifier has to follow different procedure from step (iii) onwards, which is as follows:

The first two steps would be the same, i.e.

(i) write base number 909.04;

(ii) to this add notation from Table 5

In the third step after notation of Table 5: (a) historical period may be added or (b) Areas notation may be added.

(a) When historical period is required:

(i) write base number 909.04;

(ii) add notation from Table 5;

(iii) after this add *two* zeros;

(iv) then add numbers following 909 in 909.1-909.8

Title: World history of Indians upto 19th Century

Base No.		**Table 5**		**Add**		**Nos. following 909**
909.04	+	-91411	+	00	+	[909.]81

C. No. 909.04914110081

ANALYSIS

It means if the option is choosen then in place of one zero, two zeros are to be used if historical period is required;

(b) When areas notation is required:

(i) write base number 909.04;

(ii) add notation from Table 5;

(iii) after this add *one* zero;

(iv) then add Areas notation 3-9 from Table 2

It simply means that if option is used then instead of one zero, two zeros would be used for adding historical periods and one zero which in normal practice is used to add historical periods would be used to add Areas notations from Table 2. e.g.:

Title: History of Indians in Great Britain

Base No.		Table 5		Add		Table 2
909.04	+	-91411	+	0	+	-41

C. No. 909.0491411041

(2B) WORLD HISTORY - HISTORICAL PERIODS

For general and specific historical periods readymade class numbers are enumerated, e.g.:

Modern world history

909.08

History of the 20th Century

909.82

(2C) 909.09 GENERAL WORLD HISTORY OF AREAS, REGIONS, PLACES IN GENERAL

General areas and regions for which notations are enumerated under - 1 in Table 2 are to be added after 909.09 using following steps :

(i) write base number 909.09;

(ii) add to this Areas notation following - 1 from Table 2;

(iii) then add to this number one zero if the document deals with specific period;

(iv) then add to this numbers following 909 in 901.1-909.8, e.g.:

Title: History of third world countries.

Base No.		Table 2 nos. following -1
909.09	+	[-1]724

C. No. 909.09724

Title: History of third world countries from 1970-1989

Base No.	Table 2 nos. following -1		Add		Add nos. following 909
909.09	[-1]724	+	0	+	[909.]828

C. No. 909.097240828

(3) **939-990 HISTORY OF SPECIFIC CONTINENTS, COUNTRIES, LOCALITIES; OF EXTRATERRESTRIAL WORLDS:**

For practical purposes the class numbers of History of Specific continents, countries and localities may be divided in the following manner:-

(i) 930 is allotted to Ancient World and 940 - 990 to Modern World,

(ii) Ready Made class numbers are mainly devised on the basis of historical periods and are enumerated as subdivisions, e.g.:

Title: A study of Gupta Dynasty

C. No. 934.06

Title: History of Europe during renaissance

C. No. 940.21

(iii) Class numbers devised on the basis of special Tables for 930-990 which may be added after Areas notation from Table 2, e.g.

Title : Historian of Japan

Base No.		**Table 2**		**Special Table**
9	+	52	+	007202

C. No. 952.007202

(iv) Class numbers devised on the basis of Add Device, e.g.:

Title: History and Civilization of the native races of Sikkim

Base No.		**Table 2**		**Special Table**		**Table 5**
9	+	54167	+	004	+	011

C. No. 954.167004011

In Edition 20, there are few following improvements in the enumerated subdivisions under 939–990.

(i) 939 has now seven subdivisions from 939.1-939.8 as against two subdivisions 939.1 and 939.8 in Edition 19.

(ii) Another improvement has been made in regard to use of *Add Device* in place of enumeration. For example, 940.31 has about 21 subdivisions, 940.46-.48 having more than 30 subdivisions in Edition 19, but in Edition 20 these have been replaced by Add Device.

(iii) Thirdly under many countries the historical periods have been extended to 1980 or 1990. Although historical period for India still remains at 1977.

PRACTICAL APPLICATIONS

For practical purposes the schedule for General History may be subdivided in the following manner :

(31) The wars

(32) Archaeology

(33) The ancient and the modern worlds

THE WARS

For enumerating the numbers for wars various criteria have been used by DDC. Such as the country where war began or country of one of the principle participants, etc. As ready-made class numbers are available for wars and related concepts, the classifier is, therefore, required to know only about those criteria which he may have to use while classifying a document describing wars. Few such criteria used are as follows:

1. CLASS WITH THE HISTORY OF THE COUNTRY

Class of the history of wars with the history of the country in which most of the fighting took place, e.g.:

Title: The Napoleonic War

C. No. 940.27

2. CLASS IN THE NUMBER FOR WAR

Specific battles or actions of war are to be classed in the number for war, and *Not* with the place where the action occurred. For example, any action in any country during World War II would get the number of World War II under 940.54 Military history of War, e.g.:

Title: Intelligence operations of Germany during World War II

C. No. 940.548743

(2A). Class history of specific military unit in war, e.g.:

Title: French unit in World war I

C. No. 940.41244

If number for military unit in a particular war is not available then class it in number for military operation.

(2B). Class Personal narratives of particular war in War, e.g.:

Title: Personal narratives of Indian soldiers during World War II

C. No. 940.548154

However, personal experience of war of an individual, not focused on war as such is to be classed in the subject of that individual as biography, e.g.:

Title: Personal experiences of a librarian of World War II

C. No. 020.92

(2C). If the description is about the participation of country in war then class the document in the war, e.g.:

Title: India's participation in the World War I

C. No. 940.354

3. CLASS IN THE HISTORY OF THE COUNTRY

(3A). Class routine history of every day events of an area, even if during war time in the history of the area and not in war.

(3B). Class affects of military action on everyday life and civilization of a place in the history of the place and not in War, e.g.:

Title: History of India during World War I

C. No. 954.0357

Title: Effects of World War I on the life and civilisation of India

C. No. 954.0357

ARCHAEOLOGY

ARCHAEOLOGY - GENERAL CONCEPTS

Archaeology a study of past civilization is classed under 930 History of ancient world and has been assigned the class number 930.1. Readymade class numbers are enumerated under 930.1 for miscellaneous concepts of archaeology and for specific prehistoric age, e.g.:

930.10282	Discovery of remains
930.16	Iron age

ARCHAEOLOGY OF SPECIFIC PLACES

Similar instructions are given in both Editions 19 and 20 for classifying documents relating Archaeology of specific places.

The language of the instructions in Edition 19 is not clear which has been made clear in its Manual. Similar language is used both in Manual (Ed. 19) and Edition 20 in which instruction is given under 930-939. According to this instruction :

Archaeology of all those places for which numbers are provided in 3 Ancient world (Table 2) are to be classed in the ancient world. Those places for which numbers are not available in 3 Ancient world (Table 2) are to be classed in 940-990.

Examples:

Title: Archaeology of ancient India

C. No. 934.01

Title: Archeological Studies of Australia

C. No. 994.01

Others

(1). Class archaeology of specific oceans and seas in 909.0963-909.0967, e.g. of Caribbean Sea,

(2). Class industrial archaeology in 609.

HISTORY OF SPECIFIC CONTINENTS, COUNTRIES, LOCALITIES; OF EXTRATERRESTRIAL WORLDS

Two methods are used to subdivide the history of specific continents, countries, localities and of extraterrestrial worlds:

1. Historical periods
2. Special Table

HISTORICAL PERIODS

Enumeration Device mainly is used to provide historical periods under 930-990

However, the help of Add Device, has also been taken to add numbers from the Schedules or from Tables - mainly from Table 2, e.g.:

958 Central Asia

958.5 Turkmenistan

Add to base number 958.5 the numbers following 958.407-958.408

Similar instruction is provided under 958.6 and 958.7

However, Add Device is used maximum for devising numbers for World Wars.

SPECIAL TABLE

A Special Table has been provided under 930-990. The notations of this table may be used after Areas notation from Table 2, as per instruction given therein;

Title: History and civilization of Afro-Americans in Canada

Base No.		**Areas 3-9 Table 2**		**notation from Special Table**		**Notation from Table 5**
9	+	-71	+	004	+	-96

C. No. 971.00496

Title: Indian historians and historiographers

Base No.		**Areas 3-9 Table-2**		**Notation from Special Table**
9	+	-54	+	007202

C. No. 954.007202

Practical Problems

1. History and civilization of East and South-east Asians living in Europe.
2. Columbia Lippincott Gazetteer of the World.
3. Interpretation of archaeological remains.
4. A study of travels in India during Gupta period.
5. Japan: An official guidebook of Japan Travel Bureau.
6. How to use genealogical sources.
7. World travel guides.
8. Who's who in India.
9. A comprehensive biographical dictionary of golf players.
10. 1982 Fodor's guide to the ruins of Rome.
11. Relief and welfare activities of Red Cross during World War II.
12. Royal houses of Netherlands.
13. History of the growth of Indian civilization.

14. Social, political and economic history of USA from 1861-1865.
15. A study of changing identifications on motor vehicle registration plates in India.

Solutions

1. 940.0495
2. 910.3
3. 930.10285
4. 913.4046
5. 915.204
6. 929.1
7. 910.202
8. 920.054
9. 927.96352
10. 914.563204928
11. 940.54771
12. 929.792
13. 934.03
14. 973.71
15. 929.90954

XV

PRACTICAL PROBLEMS

Exercise I - Based on ready-made class numbers:

1. Trade unions and right to strike.
2. Turtle grass.
3. Microscopy in biology.
4. Liquid particle technology
5. Robots.
6. Strategy and tactics in chess.
7. Psychology of nonliterate people.
8. Effects of prices on consumption.
9. Venus and Adonis poems by William Shakespeare.
10. Market research and analysis.
11. Transmission of sound.
12. Submarine warfare in World War I.
13. Economic cause and effects on poverty.
14. Role of United Nations in peaceful settlement of disputes.
15. Social psychology.
16. Materia medica.

Exercise II - Based on Table 1 and 2

1. Clock and watch maintenance and repairs.
2. Agricultural charts.
3. Historical research on the growth and decline of communism.
4. Weather forecasts and reports for South Asia.
5. History of South-South countries.
6. General statistics of Sri Lanka.
7. Noise pollution in Rajasthan.

8. Theory and philosophy of Indian commercial law.
9. University courses in pharmaceutical chemistry in India.
10. Management and facilities for golf in India.
11. A bibliography of books on Sikhism.
12. Organisation and management of information centres.
13. Need of equal employment opportunity programmes in India.
14. Theories of heat transfer.
15. Effects of social conditions and factors on architecture.

Exercise III - Based on Tables 1 to 4

1. Methodology used in vocational interest aptitude tests.
2. A guidebook to holy places of Germany.
3. Etymology of South Slavic languages.
4. Collections of literature by rural authors.
5. Patents for safety engineering of motor vehicles.
6. Arabic-Hindi dictionary.
7. Languages of Asia.
8. Critical analysis of the social themes described in English poetries of Victorian period.
9. Evaluation of Sociological Hindi fictions.
10. A collection of Punjabi language literature by residents of Canada.
11. Collections of drawings from Paris.
12. Historical and descriptive study of the morphology and syntax of Marathi language.
13. Dialects of Canada.
14. A study of Thai literature from 1980 to 1992.
15. Japanese prose literature of late 19th century.

Exercise IV - Based on 7 Tables and Special Table

1. Climate of Australia.

2. Chinese language collections.
3. Role of communist parties in Indian politics.
4. Migration from Bangladesh to India.
5. Recent research papers on hypertension.
6. A study of the rocks of Karakoram mountains.
7. A study of national flags.
8. Collections of literature describing mythological persons.
9. Social services to homeless people.
10. Comprehensive biographical dictionary of Bengalis.
11. Russians in India.
12. Indian legislative manuals.
13. How helpful is shock therapy in mental disorders.
14. Marino sediments of Caribbean Sea.

Exercise V - All aspects

1. Sociology of religion.
2. Cloud seeding.
3. Reviews of educational and entertainment films.
4. Astrological analysis and predictions about India and its leaders.
5. Marble mining in Rajasthan.
6. Geomorphology of Sargasso sea floor.
7. Testing the vertical lift crafts.
8. Reporting of social problems.
9. Social status of Hindi speaking people in Europe.
10. Gas chromatography.
11. An appraisal, of the work on criminal psychology.
12. Social responsibility of the management with respect to protection and preservation of environment.
13. Architectural constructions in asbestos.
14. Research in Sanskrit rhetorics.
15. Surgery of wounds and injuries of horses.

16. Need of environmental protection.
17. Radiochemistry of organometallic compounds.
18. The impact of drug culture on society.
19. List of Japanese dead during World War II.
20. Inscriptions on the paper money of India.
21. Indian school of economic thought.
22. Bird watching in European countries.
23. Pilot guides to Japan.
24. Foreign relations of China and India.
25. Damage to wheat crops by birds in India.

Solutions

Exercise I

1. 331.892
2. 584.73
3. 578
4. 620.43
5. 629.892
6. 794.12
7. 155.81
8. 339.42
9. 822.33V3
10. 658.83
11. 534.2
12. 940.451
13. 339.46
14. 341.523
15. 302
16. 615.1

Exercise II

1. 681.110288
2. 630.20122
3. 335.430722
4. 551.6554
5. 909.09724
6. 315.493
7. 363.7409544
8. 346.540701
9. 615.19071154
10. 796.35206
11. 294.6016
12. 027.006
13. 351.1040954
14. 536.2001
15. 720.103

Exercise III

1. 153.9400018
2. 263.04243
3. 491.8100142
4. 808.8991734
5. 629.20420272
6. 492.7391431
7. 409.5
8. 821.809355
9. 891.43308309
10. 891.42080971
11. 741.944631
12. 491.465
13. 427.971
14. 895.91009049
15. 894.68408

Exercise IV

1. 551.6994
2. 089.951
3. 324.254075
4. 304.85405492
5. 616.1320072
6. 552.09546
7. 929.92
8. 808.80351
9. 362.5
10. 920.00929144
11. 305.89171054
12. 328.5405
13. 616.8912
14. 551.46083365

Exercise V

1. 306.6
2. 551.6876
3. 028.137
4. 133.58954
5. 622.351209544
6. 551.46084362
7. 623.7460470287
8. 070.4493611
9. 305.79143104
10. 545.896
11. 364.30723
12. 658.408
13. 721.044995
14. 808.04912072
15. 636.108971
16. 363.7
17. 547.050458
18. 306.1
19. 940.546752
20. 769.55954
21. 330.150954
22. 598.072344
23. 629.1325452
24. 327.54051
25. 633.11968